GW00674100

A journey to
MEDIEVAL CANTERBURY

ANDY HARMSWORTH AND CANTERBURY ARCHAEOLOGICAL TRUST

A Journey to Medieval Canterbury has been written primarily as a general interest book for children in the 11 to 14 age range. Canterbury is fortunate in that many of its medieval features are still visible today for the reader to search out and enjoy. As an introduction to the subject, the book will also appeal to the interested adult looking for a lively, reliable summary.

Teachers

Much of the material is suitable for teaching parts of the National Curriculum at Key Stages 2 and 3. Individual teachers are welcome to adapt and reproduce content for use in the classroom without written permission from the copyright holders.

CONTENTS

A JOURNEY THROUGH TIME

Have you ever thought what it would have been like to live in a different time? Imagine that you had been born about 600 years ago. What would your life have been like? Would it have been any different from living at the beginning of the 21st century?

This book will help you to find out some answers to these questions. It will take you on a journey back to a time which is known as the **Middle Ages** or the **Medieval period**. It will also help you to understand how much we know about the lives of people who lived such a long time ago.

Your travels will begin in 1066 when Duke William of Normandy and his soldiers from Northern France arrived in Canterbury. You will see what the results of their arrival were for the people who lived here. Then you will find out what the lives of people who lived in Medieval Canterbury in the 12th and 13th centuries were like (from about 1100 to 1300). Exactly when your journey will finish is not so certain ....

This timeline shows you how far back in time you will be travelling:

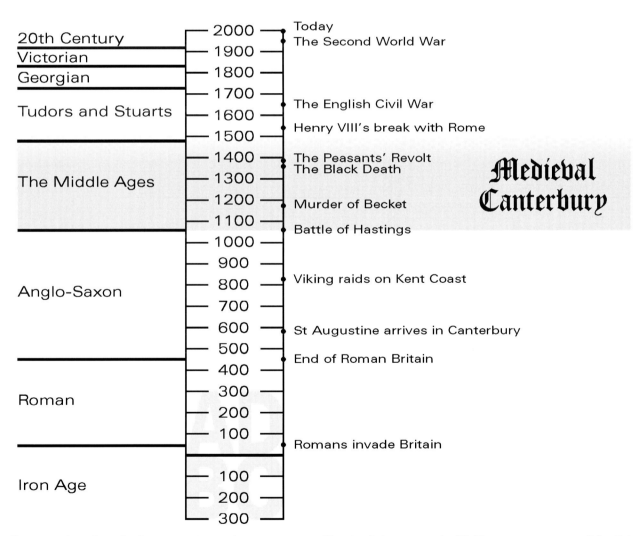

If you make plans before you start a journey, you will get a lot more out of it. To prepare yourself for this journey you need to:

• understand that the illustrations in this book are just as important as the writing. If you spend time looking closely at the details they contain you will get a lot more out of your journey

• be introduced to your 'guides' ...

HOW DO WE KNOW ABOUT MEDIEVAL CANTERBURY?

It is not easy to find out about Medieval Canterbury. It existed over 600 years ago. The people who lived here died long ago – we cannot ask them what their lives were like. There were no cameras during the Middle Ages. There are no photographs, television programmes or films for us to look at. There were no newspapers to give us news about local events. Few people in the Middle Ages could read or write. Books were written out by hand and were very expensive. So, there are not many medieval books for us to read.

All we can do today is examine the clues which have survived from such a long time ago. We call these clues **sources**. Luckily several kinds of sources about Medieval Canterbury have survived:

Medieval Documents

Historians study documents to find out all they can about the past. Written sources from the Middle Ages are called **manuscripts** because they were written by hand. One important type is **chronicles**. They are accounts of events which were written by monks, usually every year. Laws, letters and records which were kept by the king, the Church and law courts are also important written sources for historians. For example, the monks of Canterbury Cathedral kept records of all the land and buildings they owned. Historians can also study medieval maps, plans and drawings of Canterbury.

Archaeology

Historians know that many sources about Canterbury's past have not survived. Most of the buildings in which the people of Medieval Canterbury lived and worked are no longer standing. Many of them were demolished in later times so that new ones could be built. Others were burnt down in fires or destroyed by bombs during the Second World War (1939–45). Most of the things which people made, owned and used were eventually thrown away as rubbish. Sometimes however, traces of these sources can still be found under the ground.

Archaeologists try to find these 'lost' sources by digging into the ground. Sometimes they have to dig under water. They have to remove all the layers of soil very carefully so that they do not damage any clues. We call this an **excavation** or 'dig'. In this way archaeologists can uncover the buried remains of old buildings and discover **finds** such as bones, pottery, tools, coins and jewellery. They also examine the soil very carefully. Remains of seeds, pollen and insects can tell archaeologists a lot about peoples' surroundings, the crops they grew, the food they ate and how healthy they were. Even old rubbish pits and cess pits can contain important clues for archaeologists!

Archaeologists use all these clues to piece together a picture of how people used to live. This picture is rather like a jigsaw puzzle with a lot of missing pieces. When archaeologists make a new discovery they add another piece to the puzzle and slowly the picture becomes clearer.

There has been a full-time team of archaeologists in Canterbury since 1976. It is called the **Canterbury Archaeological Trust**. Most of its work comes when new building developments are planned, like roads, shops, offices and car parks.

"I am reading the Domesday Book. It was written in 1086 for William the Conqueror. It can tell us a lot about Canterbury at this time, as you will see..."

In Canterbury, archaeologists must be allowed by law to investigate any site which is to be redeveloped. If a decision is made to excavate it, they have to work very quickly. They must record all the details of what they find as accurately and thoroughly as possible before the new building work begins. As soon as the excavation is finished, the builders bring mechanical diggers and pile drivers onto the site to prepare it for the new buildings. These modern machines can destroy forever any evidence which still lies buried underground. Canterbury's archaeologists often have no second chance. That is why their work is known as **"Rescue Archaeology"**.

Standing Buildings

Historians and archaeologists also study historic buildings which are still standing today. There are still many medieval buildings in modern Canterbury. Even though they might have changed quite a lot over the centuries, they are very valuable sources about Medieval Canterbury. The most famous is Canterbury Cathedral but there are many others as you will see.

"We carried out this excavation in Canterbury in 1990. We found a lot of remains from the Middle Ages. What are each of the archaeologists doing?"

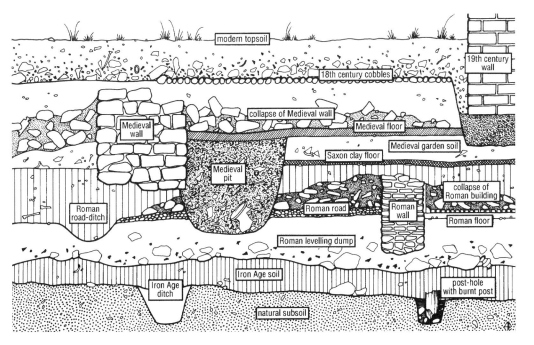

Drawn by Mark Duncan

"We find different layers as we dig underground. We know how to date the objects we find in these layers. Usually the deepest layers are the oldest ones."

You have now been introduced to the 'guides' for your journey – archaeologists and historians. They work together to discover as much as they can about Canterbury's past. The information and sources in this book come from the work they have done.

WHAT WAS CANTERBURY LIKE BEFORE THE NORMAN CONQUEST?

The Romans invaded Britain in AD 43. They found an Iron Age village where Canterbury is today. The Romans built a large town here which they called **Durovernum Cantiacorum**. You can find out more about it in our book '**Roman Canterbury**'. The Romans left Britain in about AD 450. Their town soon fell into ruins and became overgrown.

The Beginnings of Anglo-Saxon Canterbury

Then three peoples came to southern Britain from across the North Sea. They are known as the Angles, Saxons and Jutes – or more simply the **Anglo-Saxons**. During the late 5th century some of them began to settle inside the walls of the ruined Roman town. They were a farming people. They cleared the land so they could grow crops and keep animals. They built wooden houses to live and work in. Their settlement soon became the most important place in the new Kingdom of Kent. It later became the capital of Kent and was named **Cantwaraburh** (the stronghold of the people of Kent). This is where the modern name of Canterbury comes from.

St Augustine and Christianity

Ethelbert was the king of Kent at the end of the 6th century. He was the most powerful ruler in the country and spent a lot of time in Canterbury. In AD 597 **St Augustine**, a monk from Rome landed at Thanet in Kent, together with 40 other monks. They had been sent by the Pope to convert the Anglo-Saxons to the Christian religion. King Ethelbert went to Thanet to meet Augustine:

"This account of Augustine meeting King Ethelbert was written by Bede, an Anglo-Saxon monk who lived in a monastery at Jarrow, in Northumberland. He wrote his account in about AD 700."

"This picture shows St Augustine preaching to King Ethelbert. It was drawn for a school textbook in the early 20th century."

"After some days, the King came to the island and sitting down in the open air, summoned Augustine and his companions. He did not allow them to meet him in a house. He held an ancient superstition that they practised magic, and might have an opportunity to deceive and control him. But the monks had power from God, not the devil. They approached the King carrying a silver cross and a painting of our Lord and Saviour. First they said prayers to God and sang a hymn for the salvation of themselves and those for whose sake they had come. Then, at the king's command, Augustine sat down and preached the word of life to the King and his court."

King Ethelbert welcomed Augustine and allowed him to preach to the people. He also allowed him to build a small church in Canterbury. It was called **Christ Church**. This was Canterbury's first **cathedral**. Augustine became the first **Archbishop** of Canterbury. He also built a monastery outside the old Roman walls. It later became known as **St Augustine's Abbey**. King Ethelbert became a Christian and the new religion spread throughout the whole country during the next century. Canterbury, with its cathedral and archbishop, became the centre of the Christian religion in England – it has been ever since.

"We don't know much about what happened in this area after the Romans left. This drawing shows what we think the Anglo-Saxon settlement in Canterbury looked like in about AD 650. Can you see the new houses and the overgrown remains of an old Roman theatre?"
Drawn by John Atherton Bowen

The Growth of Anglo-Saxon Canterbury

Many priests and monks came to study and pray in Canterbury's new cathedral and monastery. Their work became famous all over Europe. Many craftspeople like builders, potters, bone-carvers and metalworkers came to work in the Anglo-Saxon city. Merchants and traders brought goods to sell to the inhabitants. Farmers sold their corn, vegetables and meat here. Millers built water mills along the River Stour for grinding corn into flour. Several markets were opened where people could buy and sell goods. One of them was called **Wincheap** which meant wine market. In about AD 630 Anglo-Saxon kings gave permission for a **Royal Mint** to be opened in Canterbury for making coins.

As the population of Anglo-Saxon Canterbury grew many new houses, streets and churches were built. However, several disasters hit the growing city in the 9th and early 10th centuries. **Vikings** from Denmark attacked Canterbury several times and caused a lot of damage.

"**842**: There was great slaughter in Canterbury.

851: This year came three hundred and fifty ships to the mouth of the Thames and ruined Canterbury.

1011: In this year they besieged Canterbury and captured the town. They seized the Archbishop Alphege and all those in holy orders, both men and women. Then they went to their ships taking the Archbishop with them.

1012: They went to London and on Easter Saturday became very angry with the bishop because he was not willing to offer them money. They became very drunk and on Easter Day pelted the Archbishop to death with bones and cattle's heads. One of them struck him on the back of the head with the back of an axe ... and his holy blood fell on the earth and his holy soul was sent to God's kingdom."

*"These accounts of Viking attacks on Canterbury are taken from the **Anglo-Saxon Chronicle**, a yearly record of events written at this time by Anglo-Saxon monks. It might have been written at Winchester which by then was the capital of Anglo-Saxon England."*

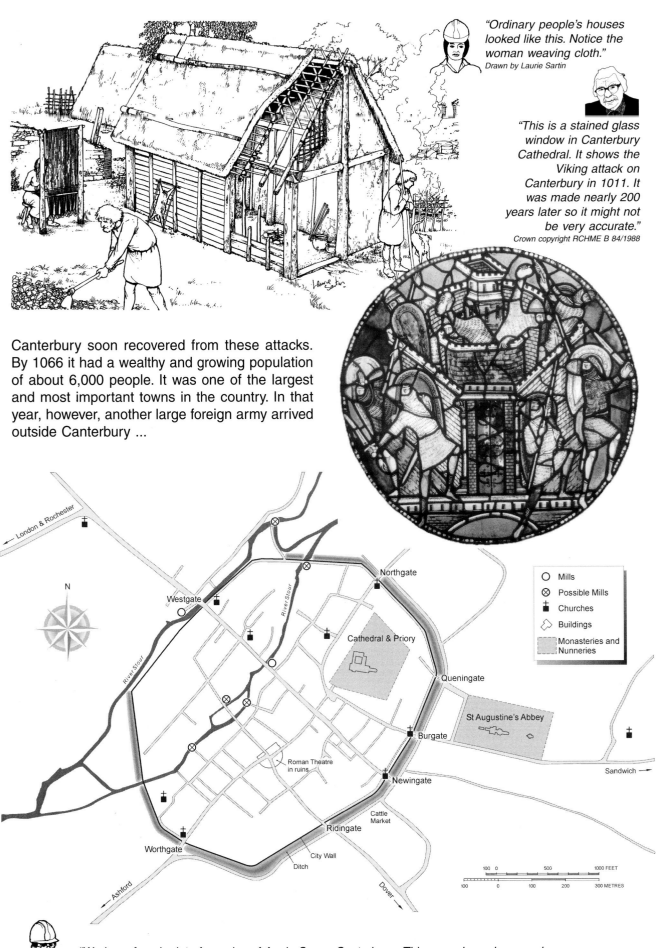

"Ordinary people's houses looked like this. Notice the woman weaving cloth." Drawn by Laurie Sartin

"This is a stained glass window in Canterbury Cathedral. It shows the Viking attack on Canterbury in 1011. It was made nearly 200 years later so it might not be very accurate." Crown copyright RCHME B 84/1988

Canterbury soon recovered from these attacks. By 1066 it had a wealthy and growing population of about 6,000 people. It was one of the largest and most important towns in the country. In that year, however, another large foreign army arrived outside Canterbury ...

London & Rochester

Westgate

Northgate

River Stour

River Stour

Cathedral & Priory

Queningate

St Augustine's Abbey

Burgate

Roman Theatre in ruins

Newingate

Sandwich →

Cattle Market

Ridingate

Worthgate

City Wall

Ditch

Ashford

Dover →

	Mills
O	Possible Mills
✛	Churches
◇	Buildings
	Monasteries and Nunneries

100 0   500   1000 FEET

100   0   100   200   300 METRES

"We have found a lot of remains of Anglo-Saxon Canterbury. This map shows how much we know about what it was like before the Norman Conquest in 1066." Drawn by Will Foster & Peter Atkinson

6

HOW DID THE NORMAN CHANGE CANTERBURY?

1066: The Normans arrive in Canterbury

In 1066 **Duke William** landed with a large army on the south coast of England. He was the ruler of **Normandy**, a powerful state in north-western France. On 14th October he won the **Battle of Hastings**. **Harold**, the last Anglo-Saxon king of England, was killed. Duke William wanted to capture London and conquer the whole country. He knew that he had to control the main towns in Kent first. After the battle he marched with his army along the south coast and captured Dover. Then he marched to Canterbury. The people quickly surrendered and William took over the city. Then William marched on to London. At the end of the year he was crowned King of England in Westminster Abbey. It took him another five years to control the whole country – then he became known as **William the Conqueror**.

Map showing the route of William's army in south east England in 1066. Drawn by Mark Duncan

"This picture of William fighting during the Battle of Hastings is from the Bayeux Tapestry. This is a long embroidery which tells the story of the Norman invasion in pictures. It was made in about 1077 for William's half-brother, Odo, the Bishop of Bayeux, to hang in his cathedral in Normandy. Some historians think that it may have been made by Anglo-Saxon needlewomen in Canterbury."

The Normans in Canterbury

Two Norman Castles

Duke William wanted to control the Anglo-Saxons as quickly as possible. Immediately he ordered his soldiers to build a **castle** in Canterbury. It was built just inside the walls where there was already an old Roman burial mound. The mound was made higher and a wooden tower was built on

the top. The Normans called this mound of earth a **motte**. Below it was a courtyard (or **bailey**) with buildings for the soldiers and stables for their horses. The bailey was surrounded by a timber wall and a deep ditch. This kind of castle is called a **motte and bailey castle**.

"This is what we think William's castle looked like in 1066. We found some clues about the castle when we excavated in this area in 1981 and again in 1988–89. The Normans called the wooden tower a donjon. We think this is why the area is known today as the Dane John Gardens. There is a high mound here which is almost certainly the remains of the motte."
Drawn by Laurie Sartin

After 1066 William built castles like this all over the country. They were made of wood and earth so they were quick and cheap to build but they were not expected to last long. In about 1090, after William's death, a new castle was built in Canterbury. It was bigger than the first castle and it was much stronger because it was built of stone. Most of the stone came from Maidstone, the Isle of Wight and Normandy. It was brought to Fordwich, Canterbury's port, by ship and then in wagons to the city. Some of the stone was probably taken from the nearby ruins of an old Roman theatre. The large stone tower or **keep** of the new castle had three floors.

The bailey was surrounded by a stone wall and ditch. Canterbury's new castle was one of the biggest castles in England at the time.

"We excavated the area around the new castle between 1975 and 1977. This is what we think it would have looked like in about 1100."
Drawn by John Atherton Bowen

Lanfranc and the Church

William also needed to control the Church. He knew that it was very important to the Anglo-Saxons. In 1070 he brought Lanfranc, a monk, over from Normandy to become the new Archbishop of Canterbury. A fire had destroyed the old Anglo-Saxon cathedral in 1067. Lanfranc replaced it with a new, larger Norman cathedral. Some of the stone was specially brought over from Normandy. He also built new cathedral **priory** (monastery) buildings for 150 monks to live in.

Lanfranc organised a lot more building work in and around Canterbury. He built a palace for himself and future archbishops to live in. It was next to the Cathedral and had a great hall, kitchens and stables. North of the city just outside the walls, he built a new monastery called **St Gregory's Priory**. A school for monks was also built there. Lanfranc also arranged for the building of two new hospitals. **St John's Hospital** was built near the new priory and had places for 60 old men and women. Just outside Canterbury, at Harbledown, he built **St Nicholas' Hospital** to care for 60 **lepers** (people who suffered from the disease leprosy).

There were also changes at St Augustine's Abbey. In 1070 the Anglo-Saxon abbot (head monk) fled. William replaced him with a Norman monk called Scotland. He demolished most of the old Anglo-Saxon buildings. Later a new, larger abbey church was built. When it was finished in 1091, the bones of St Augustine and other early archbishops were buried inside it in new tombs.

"This photograph shows you how much of the stone castle survives today."

*"This is what Lanfranc's new Cathedral probably looked like in about 1077. Parts of it were burnt down about one hundred years later and other parts were replaced. Hardly anything survives above ground today. In 1993 we carried out an excavation in the **nave** of the Cathedral and found some remains of Lanfranc's building as well as parts of the older Anglo-Saxon Cathedral."*
Drawn by Ivan Lapper

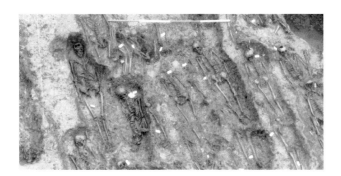

"We excavated the cemetery at St Gregory's Priory in 1989. This was a poor area in medieval times. We found almost 1,400 skeletons. Our bones specialist is studying them and will be able to tell a lot from them about medieval people – their diet, the diseases they suffered from and how old they were when they died. Many of the adults show signs of hard physical labour. Some had broken bones which had not healed well and many had arthritis. They did not clean their teeth well but people had fewer cavities than we do today."

Domesday Book

After 1066 William rewarded his Norman **barons** (lords), bishops and abbots by sharing out most of the land in England among them. In return they had to promise to be loyal to him, collect taxes and provide him with soldiers if there was a war. Then they shared out some of their land with their **knights**, who then gave small plots of land to the Anglo-Saxons. Each time people were granted land they had to make promises to obey William and the lord who granted them their land. This way of sharing out land in return for promises of loyalty and military service is called the **Feudal System**.

Twenty years later there had been so many changes that it was difficult to know how much land people had and how much it was worth. William needed to know this when he wanted more soldiers and taxes. He decided to hold a great survey to find out. In 1086 groups of royal officials were sent all over the country. Their findings were written into two large books which became known as **Domesday Book**. William died in 1087 before the work was finished.

In the city of Canterbury Edward the Confessor (an Anglo-Saxon king who died in 1066, before Harold became King) had 51 burgesses (citizens) who paid tribute (tax) and another 212 over whom he had full rights. And 3 mills at 40 shillings. Now there are 19 burgesses who pay tribute. The houses of 32 others who were there have been destroyed, 11 in the city ditch; the Archbishop has 7 of them, the Abbot of St Augustine's another 14 in exchange for the castle. There are still 212 burgesses over whom the King has full rights and the 3 mills pay 108s. The toll pays 68s. 8 acres of meadow pay 15s in tribute. 1,000 acres of woodland pays 24s. In total value, before 1066 £51, as much when **Hamo the Sheriff** (the King's tax collector) acquired it; now assessed at £50.

The burgesses had 45 houses outside the city from which they collected tribute. **Ranulf of Colombieres** holds these houses and their land from the **Bishop of Bayeux**. **Ralph of Courbepine** has 4 houses in the city which Harold's wife held. He also holds another 11 houses from the Bishop of Bayeux in the city. They belonged to Osbern Big and paid 11s 2½ d.

It was agreed about the main roads coming into the city, that whoever does wrong on them shall pay the fine to the King. If anyone makes a ditch, puts up a pigsty, narrows the road or fixes a post on any road within 3 miles of the city they shall pay a fine to the King.

In the city of Canterbury the Archbishop has 12 burgesses and 32 dwellings which the clergy hold. They pay 35s. A mill at 5s. The Archbishop holds the manor (village) of Westgate. There are 17 villagers, 83 small- holders, a church, 12 mills and farming land. To this manor before 1066 belonged 52 houses; now there are only 25 because the rest were destroyed for the Archbishop's new lodging. Its value is £40. The Archbishop holds the manor of St Martins, the Archbishop's monks hold Northgate and Hamo the Sheriff holds Nackington from the Bishop of Bayeux. The Abbot of St Augustine's holds the manor of Longport.

"This is some of the information about Canterbury which is in Domesday Book. It was originally written in Latin. Although in places it is quite difficult to understand, it tells us a lot about Canterbury in 1086 at the end of William's reign."

Canterbury in the 12th Century

Canterbury became a wealthy and growing city after the Norman Conquest. Its new cathedral, priory, abbey and other religious buildings attracted many priests, monks and nuns to preach, study and pray here. They provided many jobs for servants, cooks, clerks, carpenters and stone masons. Farmers, millers, bakers, shopkeepers, traders and craftspeople were able to sell their goods to them and their visitors. England's new kings also ruled Normandy. Trade with Normandy and other parts of Europe grew. Some merchants became very wealthy and were able to build themselves stone houses with cellars underneath. Goldsmiths opened new mints to make coins. Many people from the surrounding countryside came to live and work in the growing Norman city. Normans, Jews, Danes, and Irish came here from much further away. Many new houses were built for the growing population and by 1200 there were 22 parish churches for them. Suburbs (built-up areas outside the city walls) grew as the space inside the old Roman walls was used up. In the twelfth century Canterbury was one of the biggest towns in England.

"This coin is a penny. It has William the Conqueror's head on it and was made in Canterbury in 1087 by a moneyer called Winedi. We found it in a medieval rubbish pit near the clocktower in St George's Street in 1985."

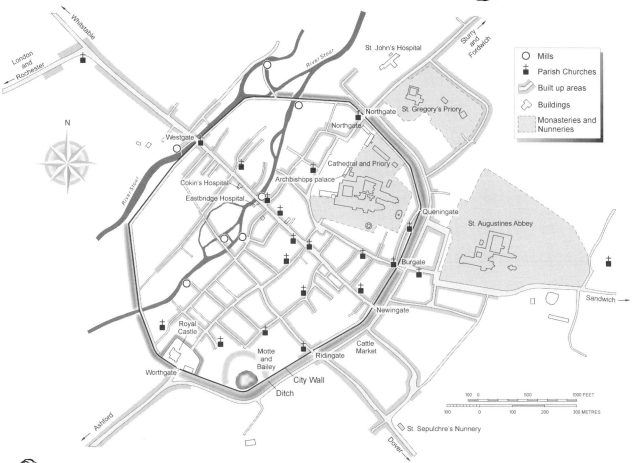

Legend:
- ○ Mills
- ✝ Parish Churches
- Built up areas
- ◇ Buildings
- Monasteries and Nunneries

"We have found many remains of Norman Canterbury in our excavations. This map shows you how much we know about what it was like in about 1200. You can compare it with the map on page 6. How much had Canterbury changed since 1066?" *Drawn by Will Foster & Peter Atkinson*

HOW DID BECKET'S MURDER AFFECT CANTERBURY?

On 29th December 1170 four knights burst into Canterbury Cathedral. They were looking for the Archbishop, Thomas Becket. What they did next brought big changes to the Norman city...

The Murder of Thomas Becket

Thomas Becket was appointed Archbishop of Canterbury by **King Henry II** in 1162. He was already the King's chief advisor and his close friend. The two men both enjoyed expensive clothes, good food and often went hunting together. King Henry wanted to have more control over the Church. He expected that his new archbishop would help him but Becket took his new job very seriously. He soon quarrelled with the King and fled to France in 1165. Henry travelled to France and the two men settled their quarrel. Becket returned to Canterbury in 1170. When he got back, Becket became angry when he heard that some barons and bishops had supported Henry during their quarrel. He decided to punish them by **excommunicating** (expelling) them from the Church. Henry was in France when he heard the news of what Becket had done. During a feast Henry is said to have shouted angrily, 'Will no-one rid me of this troublesome priest?' Four knights heard what Henry said. They immediately set off for England. They arrived in Canterbury on 29th December and headed straight for the Cathedral...

"The murderers came in full armour, with swords and axes. Some monks tried to persuade Thomas to seek safety in the Cathedral, but he would not. They then dragged him towards it.

The four knights followed quickly. The afternoon service was going on but the wicked men, with drawn swords, terrified the monks. In a spirit of mad fury, the knights called out 'Where is Thomas Becket, traitor to the King and country?'. Without fear, the Archbishop came down the steps and replied 'Here I am – a priest, not a traitor. What do you want from me?'

'You shall die this instant' they cried. He replied 'I am ready to die for my lord'. Then they rushed at him and wickedly tried to drag him out of the Cathedral to kill him. But he was holding on to a pillar. He lowered his head and lifted his hands to pray.

Then the wicked knight leapt suddenly at him and wounded him in the head. Next he received a second blow on the head, but he still stood firm. At the third blow he fell to his knees and elbows and said in a low voice 'I am ready to die for Jesus and the Church.'

The third knight wounded him terribly as he lay there. The blow cut off the top of his head, so that the white brain and red blood stained the floor of the Cathedral. The fourth knight kept away anyone who tried to interfere. A fifth man, a churchman who had come in with the knights, placed his foot on the neck of the holy priest and spattered the brains and blood around the floor. He shouted 'Come away knights, this fellow won't get up again'."

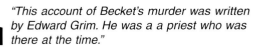
"This account of Becket's murder was written by Edward Grim. He was a a priest who was there at the time."

"This drawing of Becket's murder was made in about 1200."
By permission of The British Library HARL 5102F32

After the Murder

News of Becket's brutal murder quickly spread all over Europe. In 1173 the Pope made Becket a **saint**. In 1174 King Henry II came to Canterbury. He said that he had not wanted Becket to be killed and agreed to be whipped through the streets by the Cathedral monks as a punishment.

"This account of what happened immediately after Becket's murder was written by a monk, Benedict of Peterborough."

"While the body still lay there, some townsfolk smeared their eyes with blood. Others bought bottles and carried off secretly as much of it as they could. Others cut shreds of clothing and dipped them in the blood. Some of the blood left over was carefully collected and poured into a clean vessel and kept safely in the church. The archbishop's cloak and robe, stained with blood, were given to the poor to pray for his soul, but with inconsiderate haste they sold them for a paltry sum of money."

"Gervase was a monk at the Cathedral Priory. He saw King Henry's visit to Canterbury in 1174. This is what he wrote in his chronicle"

"On Saturday, 12th July, he walked barefoot and clad in a woollen smock all the way to the martyr's tomb. There he lay flat out for a great while in humble devotion, allowing himself to be whipped by all the bishops and abbots there present and each monk of the Church of Canterbury. There he remained, constant in prayer before the holy martyr all that day and night."

Later that year a fire destroyed the quire of the Cathedral (where the monks sang) but Becket's body in the crypt was unharmed. Many people believed that this was a sign from God.

Stories soon spread about Becket's murder. **Miracles** were said to have happened on the spot where Becket died. Pilgrims began travelling to Canterbury to pray at St Thomas' tomb. They believed that God would forgive them for their sins and cure or protect them from diseases.

In 1220 Becket's body was moved up to a beautiful new **shrine** in the Cathedral's **Trinity Chapel**. For the next 300 years thousands of pilgrims came from all over Europe to pray at Becket's shrine. These pilgrims brought a lot of wealth, business and trade to the city. Many of them left gifts of money and jewels at the Cathedral. Hospitals and inns were built nearby to provide places for them to stay. Many local people made a living by making and selling souvenirs to the pilgrims. Medieval Canterbury became rather like a busy modern tourist centre.

"This modern drawing shows what we think Becket's shrine looked like."
Drawn by Laurie Sartin © Dean and Chapter Canterbury Cathedral

WHAT WAS IT LIKE TO LIVE IN MEDIEVAL CANTERBURY?

In this part of your journey you will visit Medieval Canterbury during the **12th and 13th centuries** (from about 1100 to 1300). During this time, we know that Canterbury grew into one of the largest and most important towns in the country. By 1300 about 10,000 people lived in Canterbury. This made it the tenth largest town in England. As well as this, every year thousands of pilgrims flocked into the city. Medieval Canterbury must have been a busy, crowded and noisy place ...

We will try to help you to 'meet' some of the many different kinds of people who lived and worked in this city and find out about what their lives were like. We will use several types of sources to help you, including evidence from:

• recent archaeological excavations in Canterbury

• medieval buildings which still survive above the ground and

• medieval documents, like the records which were kept by the Cathedral monks.

However, a lot of evidence about Canterbury during this time no longer exists. For example, many medieval buildings have not survived and most of the city's written records were destroyed in 1381 during the Peasants Revolt (see page 37).

"We do not have any drawings showing what the streets and buildings of Medieval Canterbury looked like. This detail of a medieval drawing is of another town – we think that Medieval Canterbury would have looked very similar."
Mansell/Time Inc./Katz Pictures

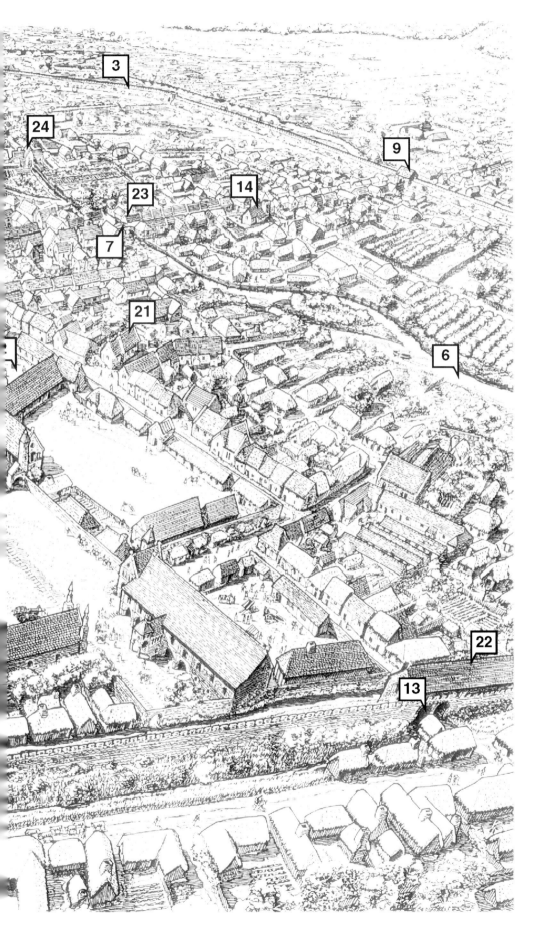

1. *Canterbury Cathedral and Priory*

2. *Archbishop's Palace*

3. *City walls*

4. *Royal castle*

5. *Remains of motte and bailey castle (Dane John mound)*

6. *River Stour*

7. *Kings Bridge and mill*

8. *High Street*

9. *Westgate*

10. *Newingate*

11. *Burgate*

12. *Ridingate*

13. *Northgate*

14. *St Peter's church*

15. *St Mary de Castro church*

16. *St John's church*

17. *St Mildred's church*

18. *St Margaret's church*

19. *St Mary Bredin church*

20. *St George's church*

21. *St Alphege church*

22. *St Mary Northgate church*

23. *Eastbridge hospital*

24. *Criene mill*

Walls, Streets and Homes

Walls and Gates

Canterbury in 1200 was surrounded by high stone walls. They had been built by the Romans nearly 1,000 years earlier. There were 6 main gates in the walls where important roads entered the city. The gates were closed at night to protect the city from attackers and robbers. Many people, however, lived in the growing suburbs outside the walls.

Streets

The streets of Medieval Canterbury were very narrow. Houses were built closely together and their upper floors hung over the street. Most streets had surfaces of trodden earth. They became muddy or flooded when it rained. There were no pavements, no street lights, no drains, no sewers and no rubbish collectors. People did not have toilets in their homes. Most of them emptied buckets and pots full of waste into the streets. Some of it was carried in open drains into the city ditch, just outside the walls, or into the river. Animals roamed along the dirty streets and rats were a common sight.

"This photograph shows what Mercery Lane, in the centre of Canterbury, looks like today. It still gives us a good idea of what medieval streets were like."

Homes

Most people lived in small huts, made of wood, mud and thatch. They had just one or two rooms. Their windows were small openings in the wall. The floor was made of earth. There was a slab of stone or tiles in the middle for a fire. They kept animals like pigs and hens in their homes. Outside they had a small plot of land for growing vegetables.

Better off people lived in bigger wooden houses. The upper floors (or **jetties**) projected out above the street. The walls were made from **wattle and daub** (wooden sticks woven together and covered with a mixture of straw, clay and animal dung). The outside of the walls were painted to make them waterproof. Most roofs were thatched. After a serious fire at the Cathedral in 1174, however, the Priory monks insisted that all nearby buildings should have tiled roofs.

The **hall** was the most important room. It was a large living room with a tiled floor and maybe tapestries on the walls. There was a **hearth** (open fireplace) in the middle. The smoke from this open fire escaped from a hole in the roof. On either side of the hall were the solar (the family's private room) and rooms where food and beer were stored. The floors of these rooms were made of packed earth, chalk, pebbles or gravel. The kitchen was usually built outside the house because of the risk of fire.

Windows in these houses were very small. Glass was far too expensive for most people. Most windows had wooden shutters which could be closed at night. Some had window-panes made from thin sheets of polished horn.

"Poorer people's houses were cheaply built. We have found very few remains of them. This is what we think they would have looked like."
Drawn by John Atherton Bowen

 "This is what these larger timber-framed houses looked like. There are many buildings like this in modern Canterbury although many of them have been altered over the centuries. Few of these surviving houses were built before the 15th century. This style of building continued into the 16th and 17th centuries."

 "This section of wattle and daub wall comes from a medieval house near Canterbury."

Only Canterbury's wealthiest citizens could afford to live in stone houses. They were very expensive. The walls were mainly built of flint and chalk. These houses usually had large stone cellars. We know from the records of the Cathedral monks that there were 30 large stone houses in Canterbury in 1200.

 "This is 53 St Peter's Street. It is the earliest medieval stone house in Canterbury. It was first built in about 1200 for Luke the Moneyer. It has been rebuilt many times over the centuries but some of its original walls are still standing. It is used as a restaurant today."

Water Supplies

The monks who lived in the Cathedral Priory and St Augustine's Abbey had piped supplies of water. Even Canterbury's wealthiest citizens could not afford such a luxury. Most of them had wells in their gardens. Most people, however, had to get water from the river, springs or public wells. It was probably very dirty.

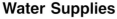

"We found the remains of this well behind St Margaret's Street in the late 1970's. It was lined with wood. There was some pottery in it which shows that this well was used during the 12th and 13th centuries."

Priests, Monks, Nuns and Friars

Religious buildings dominated Canterbury in 1200. Its cathedral, churches and monasteries were the largest buildings in the city. Many priests, monks and nuns lived and worked here. Religion touched the lives of **everybody** who lived in Medieval Canterbury.

The Roman Catholic Church

England, like every other country in Western Europe, belonged to the **Roman Catholic Church**. The Pope was the head of the Church. He lived in Rome. He appointed **archbishops** and **bishops** to help him control the Church. The Archbishop of Canterbury was in charge of the Church in England. He was also one of the King's top advisors. He owned lands all over southern England but lived at **Lambeth Palace**, near London. Sometimes he came to stay at his palace in Canterbury.

Priests and churches

Medieval Canterbury was divided into 22 areas called **parishes**. Each parish had its own church and priest. The priest held church services for local people every day. Baptisms, weddings and funerals were held in his church. He visited the sick, taught people about Christianity and told them how to live good lives so they would go to heaven when they died. Everyone in each parish had to pay a **tithe** (tenth) of their earnings to their priest.

"When people went to church, they would confess their sins to the priest. He would forgive them, if they showed that they were truly sorry. Sometimes he would make them do a penance – a punishment."

> "Priests should not have wives.
> No priest shall work for the government.
> Priests shall not spend time in inns.
> They should wear simple clothes of one colour.
> Jobs in the church shall not be sold.
> The tithe should be paid to a priest and no-one else.
> Any priest with long hair shall have it cut and shaped so that part of their ears can be seen."

"The Archbishop of Canterbury issued these rules in 1102. All priests in England had to obey them"

"This is a plan of the parish church of St Nicholas at Sturry, near Canterbury, which was probably first built in the 12th century. The

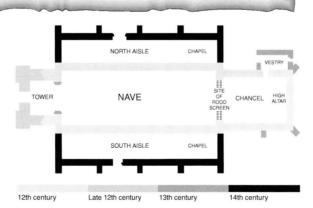

NORTH AISLE   CHAPEL

VESTRY

TOWER   NAVE   SITE OF ROOD SCREEN   CHANCEL   HIGH ALTAR

SOUTH AISLE   CHAPEL

12th century   Late 12th century   13th century   14th century

people (congregation) sat in the nave. The priest held the service from the chancel. A wooden rood screen separated the chancel from the nave. As the local population grew, parish churches got bigger. Chancels were enlarged and aisles were added. They provided more space for people to stand, for processions, for tombs where wealthy citizens were buried and private chapels where their families could pray for them. Wealthy people gave money and land to the church which helped to pay for these new buildings."

"This is a stone sink in the wall of the chapel of the Poor Priests' Hospital in Canterbury. It was called a piscina. Every church had one. The priest used it to wash his hands and holy vessels during church services."

 "Priests wore special colourful robes. The services were held in Latin. The most important service was called the Mass. The priest went to the altar. After washing his fingers, he would say prayers over wine in a silver cup and some bread on a small silver plate. At this exact moment, it was believed that the bread and wine turned into the body and blood of Jesus Christ." Drawn by Will Foster

Medieval stained glass window of the Three Magi in Canterbury Cathedral. © Dean and Chapter Canterbury Cathedral

 "Most people who went to church could not read or write. Medieval churches were beautifully decorated with wall paintings and stained glass windows. They showed stories from the Bible and what heaven and hell looked like."

The Cathedral was the most important church in Medieval Canterbury. Church services were held there every day. People from the town went to them. The nave was big enough for 5,000 people to stand in it.

13th century wall painting from the refectory in Eastbridge Hospital.

 "This is the Poor Priests' Hospital in Stour Street. In 1220 Alexander of Gloucester converted a house which was here into a hospital for old, poor and sick priests. The buildings shown in this photograph date from the 14th century, when the hospital was completely rebuilt."

Monks and Monasteries, Nuns and Nunneries

Some people wanted to live apart from everyone else so they could serve God better. Many men became **monks**. They went to live in a monastery (they were usually called **abbeys** or **priories**). Women who wanted to live similar lives became **nuns** in a **nunnery**. There were three monasteries and one nunnery in Medieval Canterbury. The Cathedral was part of **Christchurch Priory**. About 80 monks lived there. **St Augustine's Abbey, St Gregory's Priory** and **St Sepulchre's Nunnery** were just outside the city walls.

 "All monasteries were closed in the 16th century and fell into ruin. This is what we think the buildings of Christ Church Priory looked like in about 1200." Del John Atherton Bowen

1. ***Cloisters***: An open square surrounded by four covered walkways which led to the monastery's most important rooms. There were small compartments called carrels where the monks could write and study.

2. ***Cellar***: Where food was stored.

3. ***Church***: The most important building. The monks went there for church services eight times every day.

4. ***Latrines***: Toilets.

5. ***Refectory***: A dining hall, where the monks ate their meals.

6. ***Monastery Gate and wall***

7. ***Guest House***: Rooms where travellers and pilgrims could stay.

8. ***Infirmary***: A hospital for old and sick monks.

9. ***Chapter House***: All the monks met here every morning to receive instructions from the Abbot or Prior (the head monk).

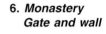

10. ***Lavatory***: Where the monks washed.

11. ***Kitchen***

12. ***Fishpond***

13. ***Monk's Graveyard***

14. ***Barn***

15. ***Bell tower***

16. ***Dormitory***: Where the monks slept. There was a **Parlour (or Warming room)** below. The monks could talk to each other in this room. There was a fire here during the winter.

17. ***Bakehouse***: Where the monks baked bread.

18. ***Brewhouse***: Where the monks brewed ale.

19. ***Almonry***: Where poor people were given food and clothes. Sometimes local people who were sick were also cared for here.

 *"Monks and nuns had to obey strict rules. They had to make three main promises: **poverty, chastity** and **obedience**. These rules were written by St Benedict, an Italian monk who lived in the 6th century. Monks and nuns had to:"*

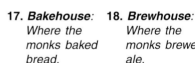

"Live in a community with no money or possessions of their own **(poverty)**
Not marry or have a girlfriend or boyfriend **(chastity)**
Obey the rules and the abbot or prior's instructions without question **(obedience)**
Be silent most of the time, especially at night
Pray in church eight times every day
Listen to a reading from the Bible or the lives of the Saints at every meal
Only have a mattress, blanket, pillow and sheet for a bed."

"Monks and nuns followed a strict daily routine. This is what their typical day was like in the winter:

2.30am	Church services (vigils and lauds)
Daybreak	Church service (prime)
8.00am	Washing, breakfast, church service (terce)
9.00am	Meeting in the Chapter House
10.00am	Work or study
12 noon	Church services (sext, Mass and none)
2.00pm	Dinner in the Refectory
2.30pm	Work or study
5.00pm	Church service (vespers) followed by supper
6.00pm	Church service (compline)
7.00pm	Bed

"This reconstruction shows the cloister at St Augustine's Abbey in the early thirteenth century. The cloister of the Cathedral Priory still looks like this today."

© English Heritage Photo Library/Jonathan Baily. Drawn by Peter Urmston

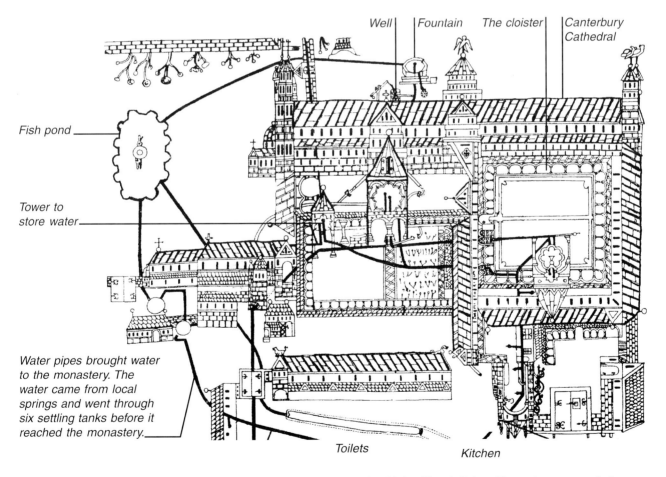

Well | Fountain | The cloister | Canterbury Cathedral

Fish pond

Tower to store water

Water pipes brought water to the monastery. The water came from local springs and went through six settling tanks before it reached the monastery.

Toilets

Kitchen

"In about 1160 Prior Wibert built a piped water supply for Christ Church Priory. The water was carried through pipes to a water tower. Then it was piped to the rooms of the priory. The dirty water was used to flush the toilets. It was one of the first piped water systems in the whole country. This plan was probably drawn in about 1165 by the engineer who designed it. St Augustine's Abbey also had a piped water supply. Its source was from springs at St Martin's Hill."

There was a lot of work to do in monasteries. The monks grew most of their own food and cooked their own meals. They kept the monastery buildings in good repair. They studied the Bible and copied out books and chronicles.

Although the monks had to live poor lives, many monasteries became very rich. Wealthy people and pilgrims gave a lot of money and land to them. By 1200 the Cathedral Priory owned about a third of all the buildings in Canterbury as well as land all over south-eastern England. People who lived there paid rent to the Priory. This money helped the monasteries to employ servants. By 1150 about 100 servants worked in the Cathedral Priory. It also helped to pay for new buildings when they were needed.

In the Middle Ages there were 12 pennies (d) in a shilling (s). There were 20 shillings in £1.

1 shilling is 5p in modern money, but prices are thousands of times higher today than they were in the Middle Ages.

	£	s	d
53 quarters of wheat (about 11,000 kg)	19	0	0
58 casks of beer (about 9,000 litres)	17	10	0
11 tuns of wine (10,000 litres)	24	0	0
20 quarters of oats (about 4,000 kg)	4	0	0
Spices	28	0	0
300 pounds of wax (about 130 kg)	8	0	0
500 pounds of almonds (about 225 kg)	3	18	0
30 oxen	27	0	0
100 pigs	16	0	0
200 sheep	30	0	0
1000 geese	16	0	0
500 fowls	6	5	0
463 chickens	3	14	0
200 sucking pigs	5	0	0
34 swans	7	0	0
600 rabbits	15	0	0
17 shields of brawn (pickled pork)	3	5	0
Partridges, mallards, bitterns, larks	18	0	0
1000 earthenware pots	0	15	0
Salt	0	10	0
1400 cups	—	—	—
3300 dishes and plates	—	—	—
Spoons and knives	8	4	0
Fish, cheese, milk, garlic	2	10	0
9,600 eggs	4	10	0
Saffron and pepper	1	14	0
Fuel, and fixing boilers and furnaces	2	8	0
300 ells of cloth (about 340m long)	4	0	0
For making tables, tressels and dressers	1	14	0
Given to the cooks and their assistants	6	0	0
Musicians	3	10	0

"Prior Wibert's water tower still survives. Some alterations were made to it in about 1400. This is what it looks like today."

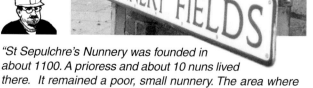
"St Sepulchre's Nunnery was founded in about 1100. A prioress and about 10 nuns lived there. It remained a poor, small nunnery. The area where it used to be is still known as Nunnery Fields today."

"This document comes from the accounts of St Augustine's Abbey. It is a list of the supplies which were bought for a huge banquet which was held there in 1309. It also shows how much they cost. The banquet was held to celebrate the appointment of a new abbot."

22

Friars and Friaries

In the early 13th century three groups of travelling preachers arrived in Canterbury. They were called **friars** (or brothers). They went out into the poorest parts of towns to teach people about the word of God. They also looked after poor and sick prople. At first they begged for food and shelter. Eventually wealthy citizens gave them money so they could build **friaries** to live in.

The first group of friars came to Canterbury in 1221. They were called **Dominicans** because they followed the teachings of a Spanish friar called St Dominic. They were also known as **Blackfriars** because they wore black robes. They did not stay long, but in 1236 another group of Blackfriars came to settle here. These were given land near the river and began to build a friary there. About 30 friars lived in it.

In 1224 nine **Franciscan** friars arrived in Canterbury. They followed the teachings of **St Francis of Assisi**, an Italian friar. They were also known as **Greyfriars**. At first they lived in rough huts on an island in the River Stour. Then in 1236 they were given some land next to the island. They began to build a friary. It contained several buildings including a church, a library and an infirmary (or hospital). About 35 Greyfriars lived there.

"Only the refectory and guest-hall of the Blackfriars still survive. This photograph shows the refectory. It was built in about 1260. Today it is used as the King's School Art Centre."

"These are some of the rules of St Francis which all Greyfriars had to obey. They were written in 1223."

"The brothers shall possess nothing for the Lord made himself poor in this world for us.

I strictly command all brothers never to receive coin or money.

All the brothers must be clothed in simple rough garments.

When they go into the world, they shall not quarrel, nor argue, nor judge others.

Let them be gentle, peaceful, modest, merciful and humble."

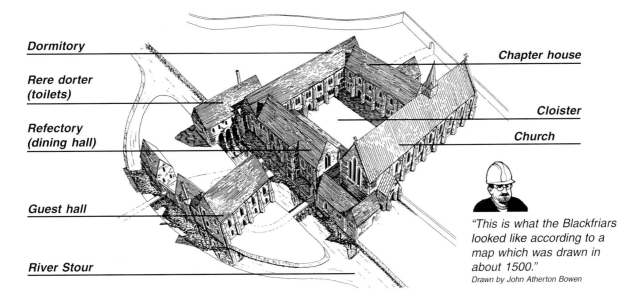

Dormitory

Rere dorter (toilets)

Refectory (dining hall)

Guest hall

River Stour

Chapter house

Cloister

Church

"This is what the Blackfriars looked like according to a map which was drawn in about 1500."
Drawn by John Atherton Bowen

"This is the only part of the Greyfriars which still survives. As you can see it was built over the river. We think it was probably the guest-room."

Another group of friars arrived in Canterbury soon afterwards. They were the **Augustinians** or **Whitefriars**. They built a friary for 18 friars near the High Street on land between Ridingate and St George's Gate. It consisted of several buildings, probably including a church, a library, dormitory, refectory and guest room.

"None of the Whitefriars' buildings survive above ground. Their remains lie beneath the 'Whitefriars Shopping Centre' as it looks here in 2001. This whole area is now being redeveloped. Already we have excavated the friary church walls. We may still be digging here while you are reading this book!"

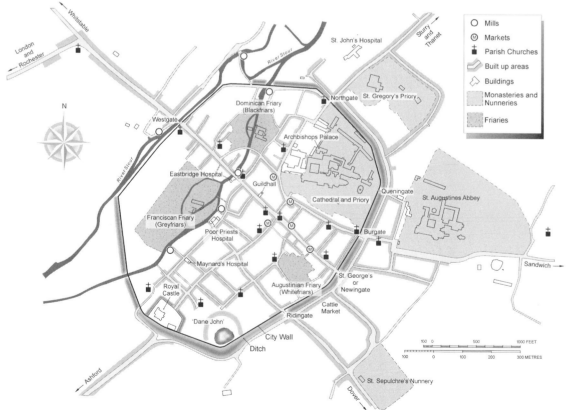

"This map of Medieval Canterbury in about 1500 is based on buildings from the time which are still standing and remains of other buildings which we have found. You can see how important religious buildings were in the medieval city. Most of the streets in modern Canterbury still follow the same routes."
Drawn by Will Foster & Peter Atkinson

Craftspeople, Shopkeepers and Traders

Many people in Medieval Canterbury made a living by making goods and then selling them to other people. These craftspeople usually worked in small workshops, in their own homes. Their goods were sold in shops, from stalls in the streets or in the city's markets and fairs. By 1234 there were about 200 shops in the city centre. Most of these were along the Parade, Mercery Lane and High Street.

Potters

Several potters worked in Medieval Canterbury. They made jugs, bowls, cooking pots, storage jars, frying pans, floor tiles and roof tiles. They used local clay and shaped it by hand. Sometimes they finished off the pot on a potter's wheel. Then they baked (or 'fired') it in a **kiln** (oven). Most pots were plain but some were decorated. The potters painted them with white paint or made imprints with their hands, thumb-nails or pointed tools. Decorated pots were more expensive than plain pottery.

After about 1150, potters learnt how to **glaze** their pottery and fire it to a higher temperature. Covering a pot with a glaze (a mixture of powdered lead and fine clay) before it was baked gave the finished pots an attractive shiny surface and made them more hardwearing and waterproof.

The most important medieval pottery industry in Kent was at **Tyler Hill**, two miles north-west of Canterbury. There were good supplies of clay, water and timber there. Archaeologists have found several remains of these potters' workshops and kilns.

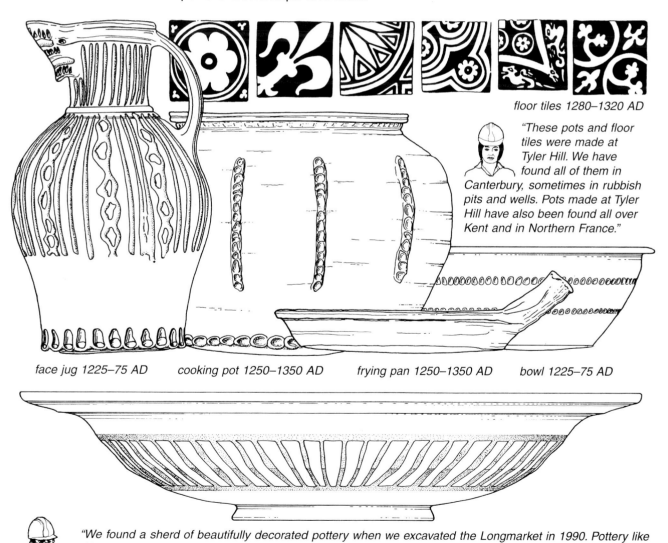

floor tiles 1280–1320 AD

"These pots and floor tiles were made at Tyler Hill. We have found all of them in Canterbury, sometimes in rubbish pits and wells. Pots made at Tyler Hill have also been found all over Kent and in Northern France."

face jug 1225–75 AD   *cooking pot 1250–1350 AD*   *frying pan 1250–1350 AD*   *bowl 1225–75 AD*

"We found a sherd of beautifully decorated pottery when we excavated the Longmarket in 1990. Pottery like this would have been expensive to buy. We know that it was made in Spain or North Africa. It could have been brought to Canterbury by a trader or someone returning from a foreign journey." *Drawings by Dominique Bacon*

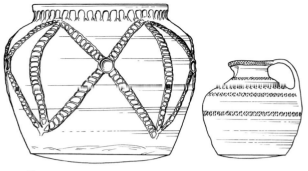

 "In 1986 we found the remains of a kiln in Pound Lane. We also found 15,000 **sherds** (pieces of broken pottery). We think this pottery was made between the 1140's and 1170's. It was glazed and made on a potter's wheel. Some of it was decorated. It was much better than the pottery which was made at Tyler Hill at this time. We think that these pots were made by a Norman potter. He might have come to Canterbury to make expensive pottery for the Cathedral monks." *Drawn by Sue Hodgkins*

"We found the remains of this 12th century potter's kiln when we were excavating at Pound Lane in 1986."

Millers

Millers bought corn from local farmers and ground it to make flour. They rented their mill from a lord like the Abbot of St Augustine's Abbey or the Archbishop. There were at least 8 mills in Medieval Canterbury along the River Stour.

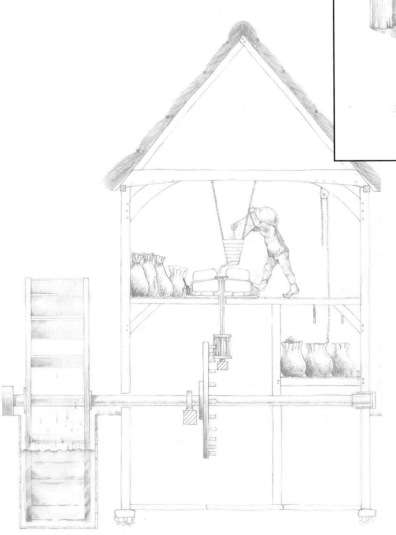

"We know that some people in Medieval Canterbury made flour in their own homes. They ground the corn by hand between two small stones called quern stones. We found one of these stones in the remains of a house in Burgate."

 "All of the mills in Medieval Canterbury were water mills. They had large water-wheels which were turned by the flow of the River Stour. This turned two large flat stones inside the mill. The miller fed the corn into a small gap between the two stones. As the stones turned in opposite directions, the corn was ground into flour. Then the miller packed the flour into large sacks, ready to sell."
Drawings by Will Foster

Bakers

Bread was the basic food of everyone in Medieval Canterbury. Several bakers worked in the town. They bought their flour from the millers. To make a loaf of bread they mixed the flour with water and yeast to make a dough. Then they left it in a warm place to rise before they baked it in an oven. As well as baking bread, they also made pies, cakes and buns. Some bakers had their own shops, others worked in the bakehouses of Canterbury's monasteries.

 "We found these remains of a medieval bread oven when we were excavating in Burgate in 1948–50. It was made of tiles set in clay. It probably dates from the 14th century."

"This medieval drawing shows bakers baking bread in their oven."

Spinners and Weavers

Many people in Medieval Canterbury made a living by making woollen cloth. After they bought the wool from a farmer or merchant, they washed it and **carded** (combed) it to separate the fibres. Then the fibres were spun on a **spindle** to make a tightly twisted yarn. This work was usually done by women in their homes. Then men took over. They wove the yarn into cloth on a loom. Then they dyed it and, in a process called **fulling**, beat it in water to shrink the cloth and make it thicker. Lastly they spread out the finished cloth to dry.

 "This medieval drawing shows men dying cloth. Most dyes came from plants which grew locally."
By permission of The British Library Roy !5 E111

Mercers

Mercers were traders who sold cloth and silk. Silk came from countries around the Mediterranean Sea and China. It was very expensive. There is still a street in Canterbury today called Mercery Lane. We know that several mercers lived in this street in the early 13th century.

 "We know quite a lot about one mercer who lived in the 12th century. Solomon the Mercer rented a building at the end of Mercery Lane. We know that his wife was called Godeleva and they had a daughter, Cecilia."

 "This medieval drawing shows cloth being made on a loom. It is unusual because it shows a woman weaving. Most weavers were men."
By permission of The British Library Eg 1894

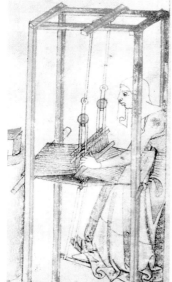

Masons

Masons were people who worked with stone. They built buildings like castles, cathedrals and monasteries. Masons had to train for many years. They usually travelled from job to job and worked all day, from sunrise to sunset. Some masons cut and shaped blocks of stone for the walls of buildings. Others carved stone to make pillars, statues and decoration around doorways and windows. They set the stones in place with **mortar** (a kind of cement made from sand and lime). Masons often had to work high up on wooden scaffolding. The stone was lifted up to them in baskets, using cranes and pulleys. The most important masons were called **master masons**. They designed buildings, were in charge of the work and supervised all the workmen. Some of them became very famous.

"This drawing of masons and carpenters at work was made in the 13th century. You can see the different kinds of tools and equipment they used."

"These holes in the city wall can be seen in many medieval buildings. They are called putlog holes. Wooden poles were put into them to hold up the scaffolding which the masons used when they constructed a building."

"Among the architects there was one, William of Sens. He was a man of great abilities. He made ingenious machines for loading and unloading ships, and for drawing mortar and stones. He delivered to the masons models for cutting the stones and made many other preparations. Both the gallery and the upper windows being finished, while he was preparing his machines for turning the great arch, at the beginning of the fifth year, the scaffold suddenly gave way, and he fell to the ground from the height of the upper arch, which is fifty feet. Being grievously bruised, he was utterly unable to attend to the work."

"Most masons could not write. They had their own mark which they chiselled into each block of stone they carved. This was so that the master mason could check how much work they had done. Then he could work out how much to pay them. These marks are all from Canterbury Cathedral." Drawn by Mark Duncan

*"In 1174 a serious fire badly damaged Canterbury Cathedral. A French master mason, **William of Sens**, was chosen for the rebuilding work. This description of him and the accident he suffered in 1179 was written by the Cathedral chronicler, **Gervase**."*

 "After William of Sens' injury, his work was completed by another mason –William the Englishman. The work was completed in about 1184 and can be seen in this photograph of the cathedral quire. It was one of the first buildings in this country to contain pointed arches. They are much stronger than round arches. They made it possible to build thinner walls, bigger windows, tall, thin pillars and high stone roofs (called vaults). This was the beginning of a new style of building called Gothic. It became the main style of architecture in the whole country for the next 350 years."

Metalworkers

There were several metalworkers in Medieval Canterbury. Most of them worked with iron. They made a range of goods including pins, knives, door locks and keys, hinges, swords, axes and horse-shoes. Sometimes they heated the iron until it was red-hot and then hammered it into shape. Other goods were made by heating the iron in a crucible until it melted. Then the molten iron was poured into a mould and left to cool.

"These metalworkers crucibles were found in St George's Street (1947) and St Margaret's Street (1982)."

"This is what we think a tanner's workshop would have looked like in the Middle Ages."
Drawn by Will Foster

"Leather usually rots when it is in the ground. We have only found a few fragments of leather goods during our excavations. This reconstruction of a medieval shoe is based on what we have found."
On view at Canterbury Heritage Museum

Tanners and Leatherworkers

Leather goods were made in Medieval Canterbury. Farmers delivered animal skins to the **tanners**. First they cleaned the skins to remove any fat and blood. Then they soaked them in large vats containing a mixture of alum and salt. The skins were trodden for 5 hours in the vats to toughen them before they were cleaned. Then the tanned skins were sold to the leatherworkers. They cut and stitched the leather to make shoes, belts, saddles, gloves and breeches (trousers).

Butchers

Many butchers worked in the city. They bought pigs, cows, sheep and chicken from the farmers and cut them up to make joints of meat. They often left their waste in the streets or threw it into the river. This attracted rats.

"This area outside the entrance to the cathedral was known as the Bullstake in the Middle Ages. Animals were tied to a post and attacked by dogs. People thought that this made the meat of the animals more tender!"
Drawn by John Atherton Bowen

Shopkeepers

At first Medieval Canterbury's craftspeople and traders sold their goods from temporary stalls in the streets and the city's weekly markets. By the 12th century, many of them had their own shops in the High Street or close by. The land here was expensive so shops were usually very narrow buildings. Medieval shopkeepers did not have large glass windows for displaying their goods like shops today. They had wooden shutters instead. They locked them up at night but used them as display counters during the day. Behind the counter was the workshop where customers could see the goods being made or prepared. The shopkeeper's main living area was behind the workshop and the bedrooms were upstairs. There were storehouses, extra workshops and a small garden or yard behind the building. Shops which sold the same goods were often grouped together in the same street.

Markets and Fairs

Local farmers and traders came into Canterbury every week to sell their produce in the city's markets. There was a cattle market outside the city wall near Riding Gate. A wine market was held in Wincheap. There was a corn market in the High Street. Nearby was the Rushmarket where baskets were sold.

Fairs were held in the city every year. Merchants from all over Europe came to sell luxury goods like jewels, silks and spices. Plays were performed and there was dancing, singing and bear baiting. Poor people could not afford to buy much but enjoyed the entertainments.

The Poor

Most of Medieval Canterbury's traders and craftspeople were not very well off, but they were not the poorest people in the city. People who worked as servants for wealthy citizens and in the monasteries did not earn much money. The poorest people of all were those who had no work. We don't know how many there were. All they could do was go to the monasteries for gifts of food and clothing or beg in the streets. Few traces of these people's lives have survived, so we know very little about them.

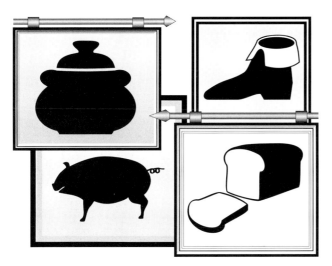

"Few people could read in the Middle Ages. Shops usually had painted signs like these hanging outside them. They told people what kinds of goods were sold in the shop. Can you tell what kinds of shops had these signs?"

Goldsmiths and Moneyers

Goldsmiths and moneyers were the wealthiest citizens in Medieval Canterbury. We know of 12 goldsmiths who lived and worked in 12th century Canterbury. They made gold and silver cups, plates, candlesticks and jewellery. Only Canterbury's wealthiest citizens and the monasteries could afford to buy their goods.

"We found the remains of this stone house when we excavated the Longmarket in 1990. It belonged to Terric the Goldsmith in about 1200. He owned several other buildings in Canterbury. In the remains of another building behind the house, we found a burnt clay floor, some crucibles for melting gold and silver and traces of ovens and furnaces. We think that this must have been his workshop."

Moneyers were people who struck coins under licence from the King. There were only three towns in 13th century England which were allowed to make coins – London, York and Canterbury. There were eight **mints** (places where coins were made) in Medieval Canterbury.

"These silver pennies were made in Canterbury between 1282 and 1289, during Edward I's reign. We found over 400 of them in a field in Wingham, near Canterbury, in 1990. They were probably buried there in a leather bag or a wooden box. It is a mystery who buried them and why."

"Lambin Frese was one of the moneyers in Medieval Canterbury. He had a workshop near the Cathedral. Sparks from the furnace in his workshop are thought to have caused the fire which destroyed part of the Cathedral in 1174. Afterwards, the monks gave him money and land to move away from the Cathedral. He built a new house and workshop near the river in Stour Street. His house later became the Poor Priests' Hospital."

A small community of Jews lived in Medieval Canterbury. They came here after the Norman Conquest. They lived in the area around Stour Street, where there is still a street today called 'Jewry Lane'. There was a synagogue nearby where they went to pray. The Catholic Church did not allow Jews to own land or work in a trade, but Jews were allowed to lend people money and charge them interest. Some of them were also moneyers. Canterbury's Jews became very wealthy. In other towns they became very unpopular. In 1290 King Edward I expelled all the Jews from the country.

Thousands of pilgrims visited Medieval Canterbury every year. In 1220 about 100,000 pilgrims came to visit Becket's new shrine in the Cathedral. Many local people made a living by selling goods to the pilgrims and providing them with places to stay. There were also free lodgings for poor pilgrims.

 "This is the Eastbridge Hospital in Canterbury. It was opened in about 1180 as a place for poor pilgrims to stay when they came to visit Becket's tomb. In this room they would have slept on beds of straw on the floor. There was also a dining room and a chapel."

 "When pilgrims entered the Cathedral a monk sprinkled them with holy water. Then they walked through the nave to these steps which led to Becket's shrine. They crawled on their knees up these steps. Over the centuries, the knees of hundreds of thousands of pilgrims wore the steps down. This photograph shows how worn the steps still are today."

 "This casket was made in about 1200. It contained some relics of Thomas Becket – pieces of his hair and some of his bones. It has pictures of Becket's murder and angels helping his soul go to heaven."
V&A Picture Library.

"The canopy was lifted and we saw inestimable treasures, the very least valuable portion was gold. Every part glistened and shone and sparkled with rare and very large jewels some of them bigger than a goose's egg."

"Erasmus, a Dutch scholar visited Canterbury in about 1513. He saw Becket's shrine and wrote this description of it."

 "Many traders sold souvenirs to the pilgrims from their shops and stalls in the streets. Lead medallions, badges and small bottles of holy water like these have been found all over Europe."

Bailiffs, Aldermen, Guilds and Mayors

People who lived in towns had to obey the King's laws and pay his taxes. At first, the King sent his own men to the towns to make sure that this was done. Gradually, however, townspeople bargained with kings to let them control more of their own affairs. Kings issued **charters** giving them special privileges – like the right to make local laws, hold law courts, collect taxes and elect their own officials.

In 1236 King Henry III issued a charter to Canterbury. It allowed the city to collect its own taxes and control its own law court. Wealthy citizens elected two **bailiffs** and six **aldermen**. The bailiffs were in overall charge of the city's affairs. The aldermen appointed night watchmen to patrol the streets, especially at night after the city gates were closed. The city's law court met every fortnight. It was called the **Burmote** (town meeting). Its members were the two bailiffs and six aldermen with 12 judges and 16 councillors. They could send criminals to the city gaol in the castle. Eventually, in 1448, the bailiffs were replaced with an elected **Lord Mayor**.

"This is the Burmote horn. It dates from at least the 13th century. It was blown when the Burmote met and also in emergencies. It is still used today when a new mayor is appointed."

"This is taken from the records of the Burmote in 1272."

"Gunnora atte Gate: sent to prison for striking, insulting and throwing stones at Richard Folkere.
John of Bread Street in London, and his friends Simon Barkysdale, William and Alice Chapman, condemned to the pillory for being pickpockets."

The King also allowed craftsmen and traders to set up **guilds**. There were several of them in Medieval Canterbury. These organisations made rules to control the quality and prices of goods made by their members. They looked after sick and old members. They made sure that **apprentices** (young people, usually boys, who were learning a trade) were trained properly. Anyone who worked in a particular craft or trade like carpenters, shoemakers and goldsmiths had to belong to their own guild. The guilds became very wealthy and powerful.

"The Burmote built a hall to meet in. Eventually it became known as the Guildhall. This photograph shows the 18th century Guildhall. The city council met there until 1949. It was demolished in 1952. There is still a 'Guildhall Street' in Canterbury today."
Canterbury Reference Library

WHEN DID MEDIEVAL CANTERBURY END?

Historians and archaeologists have different ideas about when the Middle Ages ended. The last part of your journey is through nearly 250 years of Canterbury's history, from about 1300 until the middle of the 16th century. Then you will have to decide when a journey to Medieval Canterbury should finish.

The Black Death

By the beginning of the 14th century about 8,000 people lived in Canterbury. In 1348 however, a serious outbreak of plague reached the city. It was called the **Black Death**. This disease was carried by fleas which lived in the fur of black rats. Nobody knew this at the time. Some people believed that it was a punishment from God. They prayed and went on pilgrimages. Others thought that it was to do with the position of the planets or 'bad air'. Nobody could do anything to stop this frightening disease. It spread rapidly and about half of the people in Canterbury died. Medieval documents tell us that there was also bad weather at this time. Crops failed to grow so people had less food to eat. This must have made people's lives even more difficult.

The Black Death lasted for a year but there were many more outbreaks of plague and other diseases in Canterbury during the next century. Houses were left empty, landlords lost money and several parish churches had to be closed. By 1500 Canterbury's population had fallen to just 3,000 people.

"*God often allows plagues, famines, conflicts, wars and other forms of suffering, and uses them to terrify and torment men in order to drive out their sins. This is why England, because of the growing pride and corruption of its people, and their numberless sins, is to be oppressed (punished) by the pestilence (disease).*"

"*This is part of a letter which the Prior (head monk) at Canterbury Cathedral wrote to the Bishop of London in September 1348.*"

"*People first knew they had caught the plague when swellings appeared in their groin and armpits. Some of them were as large as apples or eggs. From these two parts of the body the boils spread out. Then black spots appeared on the arms and thighs. These quickly led to death.*"

"*The Black Death spread all over Europe. We think that it killed millions of people – probably about one person in three. This description of the disease was written in 1353 by an Italian poet.*"

1198 RALPH. *"Radulphus" Probably the one styled "nepote beati Thome Mart" "nephew of the blessed Thomas the Martyr*	1494 THO
	1512 Dᴿ R
	1535 Dᴿ
	1538 WIL
	1565 WIL
1233 THOMAS ᴏꜰ WYLTON	1569 Dᴿ T
1236 PETER	Ca
1242 JOHN ᴏꜰ SUFFOLK	1595 Dᴿ F
1261 GEOFFREY	Bis
1264 WALTER	1596 ISA
1280 HAMO	1597 Dᴿ
1284 JOHN	De
1299 WILLIAM BURGESS	1625 RO
1321 JOHN KENTYNG	1628 JO
1323 JOHN ᴏꜰ THYNGEN	1664 EDᵂ
1334 RICHARD ᴏꜰ IVYNGHO	Ca
1342 ROGER ᴏꜰ RONDES	1673 Dᴿ
1349 MATTHEW ASSHETON	Late
1349 WILLIAM ᴏꜰ FAREHAM	1688 Dᴿ.
1351 WILLIAM ᴏꜰ BRADELE	Ara
1351 THOMAS NEWE	1708 JO
1379 ROBERT ᴏꜰ BRADEGAR	Master of S
1380 JOHN OVYNG	1709 JO
1382 JOHN LUDHAM	1719 JO
1383 JOHN WHITTECLYFF	A
1383 WILLIAM CAUSTON	1746 JO
1395 JOHN MONTAGUE	1753 HE
1400 THOMAS PELLYCAN	1777 Dᴿ
1405 THOMAS BURTON	An
1429 JOHN STOPYNDON	1789 W
1437 JOHN NEEL	1803 Al
1442 THOMAS KEMP *Archdeacon*	1823 JO
1445 Dᴿ THOMAS CHICHELEY *Archdeacon & nephew of Archbishop*	1850 W
	1887 Th
1467 JOHN BOURCHIER *Archdeacon*	1899 A

"*This is a list of the Masters of the Eastbridge Hospital. Can you tell whether this hospital was affected by the Black Death?*"

New Defences

Canterbury's walls and gates were over 1,000 years old by the time of the Black Death. They were in a bad condition. Over the centuries people had robbed stone from the walls and the ditches had become full of mud and rubbish. It became urgent to strengthen Canterbury's defences when war with France broke out in 1369.

Work began to rebuild the **Westgate** in 1380. The Archbishop of Canterbury, **Simon Sudbury**, paid for most of the work but local people also had to pay extra **taxes**. By about 1400 all of Canterbury's walls and gates had been repaired or rebuilt. Twenty four new towers were built at intervals along them.

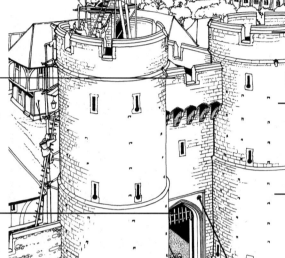

"This is what we think the new Westgate looked like in about 1400. It was used as the city prison for nearly 500 years." Drawn by Laurie Sartin

A **machicolation** or overhanging stone gallery. From here boiling water or tar could be poured on enemy soldiers who tried to break down the doors.

A **portcullis** (a heavy metal grill). This would be lowered to protect the two heavy oak doors behind it.

Gunloops. Guns were coming into use in the late 14th century. Soldiers could fire guns through these keyhole shaped holes. The Westgate is one of the first buildings in Britain which was equipped for guns.

Battlements to protect soldiers when they fired arrows at attackers.

The **stone** was brought to Canterbury from Maidstone, over 30 miles away.

Two **round towers**. Round towers became popular from the 13th century onwards. They were stronger than square towers and there were no corners for attackers to chip away at.

A **drawbridge**. This could be raised if there was an attack.

"Canterbury had six gates in the Middle Ages, but only the Westgate has survived. This is what it looks like today."

"Several sections of Canterbury's walls were destroyed in the 17th century. This is one of the best parts which survives today. Behind it you can see the Dane John Mound where William the Conqueror built his first castle in Canterbury in 1066."

The Peasants' Revolt, 1381

Drawn by Will Foster

In the summer of 1381 thousands of peasants all over south-eastern England rose up in protest against the government. They particularly hated the Archbishop of Canterbury, Simon Sudbury. He had advised the young King, Richard II, to make everyone pay a poll tax of 1 shilling (5p). This was more than a day's wages for a peasant. Wat Tyler led a band of angry peasants into Canterbury. They attacked the castle, burnt all the records which were kept there and freed the prisoners. They forced their way into the Archbishop's Palace and stole many valuable goods. You can read what they did next in this document:

"Four thousand of the rebels entered Canterbury Cathedral during a service. They knelt down and then demanded that the monks must elect a new Archbishop of Canterbury. They said 'He who is archbishop now is a traitor and will be beheaded for his sins.'

And when they had done this, they joined their supporters in the town. Then they summoned the mayor and townsfolk and asked if they would swear to be faithful and loyal to King Richard and the loyal commons of England. The mayor agreed to this, so they swore the oath. The rebels then asked if there were any traitors in Canterbury. Three names were mentioned and these people were immediately dragged out of their houses by the rebels and beheaded. After this the rebels left guards in Canterbury and then marched towards London with five hundred townsfolk who had joined them."

When the peasants reached London they burst into the Tower of London and murdered Archbishop Sudbury. Soon afterwards Wat Tyler was killed and the peasants went home. Later that year the King came to Canterbury and

*"This account comes from the **Anominalle** (anonymous) **Chronicle**. We don't know who wrote it, but we think that it was written at the time by someone who saw what happened."*

"This drawing shows the rebels murdering the Archbishop of Canterbury and the King's Treasurer in the Tower of London. It was drawn in about 1460."

several supporters of the revolt were executed. Although the peasants were defeated, the poll tax was never collected again. Landlords faced a shortage of peasants to work for them and by 1500 most of the demands of the Peasants' Revolt had been met.

Pilgrimages

Huge numbers of pilgrims continued to come to Canterbury during the 14th century. Several new inns were built close to the Cathedral to provide more places for them to stay. The most famous was

"The Bull Inn was built for pilgrims in the middle of the 15th century. It had shops on the ground floor."

"Most of the Cheker of the Hope was destroyed by fire in the 19th century. Part of the ground floor survived because it was built of stone. You can see the stone arches of the original building in this modern photograph."

Geoffrey Chaucer

Geoffrey Chaucer was born in London in 1343. He spent most of his life working for the government. In about 1385 he began to write a long poem about a group of 30 pilgrims who were travelling from London to Canterbury. It described the stories they told to each other during their journey. Chaucer wanted each pilgrim to tell 4 stories. He had only finished 24 of them when he died in 1400. He called them 'The Canterbury Tales'. Although it was not finished, Chaucer's book is one of the most important books in the English language. It was one of the first books to be written in English rather than Latin. It is still very popular today.

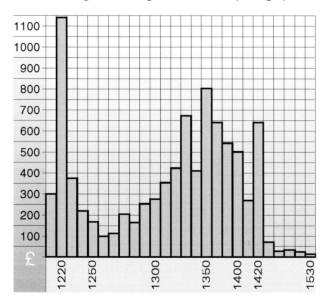

"We wanted to find out how many pilgrims visited Becket's shrine during the Middle Ages. We have worked out how much money they gave to the Cathedral between about 1200 and the 1530's. As you can see the amount became much smaller after 1420. This makes us think that far fewer pilgrims visited Canterbury after 1420 – but we do not really know why."

the **Cheker of the Hope**. It was built by the Cathedral Priory in 1392–5 and cost over £862. It was mainly built of wood. It had a cellar, a ground floor of shops, two floors of dormitories and private rooms, a large central courtyard and windows painted in gold. Two other large pilgrim inns, the Sun Inn and the Bull Inn, were built close to the Cathedral gate in the 15th century.

Canterbury Cathedral: Buildings and Burials

By the end of the 14th century several parts of the old Norman Cathedral and Priory were in a bad condition. In 1377 the Norman nave was demolished and Henry Yevele, the King's master mason, began work on a magnificent large new nave. There was an earthquake in Canterbury in 1382 which may have held up the work, but the new nave was finished in 1405. A new cloister was also built in the Priory. In 1450 a carved stone screen, decorated with statues, was built to separate the quire (where the monks sang) from the nave. A new central tower, known as Bell Harry, was completed by 1500.

Kings and Queens were usually buried in Westminster Abbey, but many important people like archbishops and nobles were buried in Canterbury Cathedral. During the later Middle Ages there were two important royal burials in the Cathedral. Both of them were very close to Becket's shrine. In 1376 Edward, the Black Prince, was buried underneath a grand tomb with his armour and weapons hung around it. He was the eldest son of King Edward III and became famous for defeating the French at the Battle of Crecy in 1346. In 1437 King Henry IV was buried here, 24 years after his death – he is the only medieval king who is buried in Canterbury Cathedral.

*"Henry Yevele's nave still survives today. It was built in a new style called Perpendicular which means upright straight lines – you can see why in this photograph. You can also see the later stone screen or **pulpitum** at the end."*

1485 – the end of the Middle Ages?

In 1485 Henry VII, the first of the Tudors, became King of England. The Middle Ages is often thought to have finished when the Tudors came to the throne. Did it bring Medieval Canterbury to an end?

There were no dramatic changes in Canterbury for many years after 1485. Life under the new king was much the same as before. The improvements to the city's defences were finally completed with the rebuilding of St George's Gate and Burgate. Building work at the Cathedral continued. In 1521 **Christ Church Gate**, a grand new entrance to the Cathedral precincts, was finished. Big changes, however, did come to Canterbury during the reign of Henry's son, Henry VIII ...

"This is the tomb of King Henry IV in Canterbury Cathedral. In 1832 the tomb was opened up. It is said that the King's head and beard were well preserved and his face was still recognisable!"

"This is Christ Church Gate which was finished in 1521. It was built to commemorate the marriage of Prince Arthur, Henry VII's eldest son, to Catherine of Aragon, a Spanish princess (after Arthur died she married his brother Henry VIII). The statue of Jesus was added recently. An earlier statue had been there until it was destroyed during the Civil War of the 17th century. To the right you can see the remains of the Sun Inn, a 15th century pilgrims' inn. Behind is Bell Harry Tower which was finished by 1500."

 "Here you can see part of the remains of St George's Gate. It was built at the end of the 15th century. We found these remains during an excavation in 1988."

CHRISTCHURCH GATE

ENTRANCE TO CATHEDRAL

SUN INN

BULL INN

MARKET CROSS

GUILD HALL

THE CHEKER OF THE HOPE INN

MERCERY LANE

HIGH STREET

ST MARY BREDMAN CHURCH

ST ANDREW'S CHURCH

 "This is what we think the centre of Canterbury looked like in about 1520."
Drawn by John Atherton Bowen

"The shrine was built of stone up to a man's height and then upwards of timber. Inside was an iron chest which contained the bones of Thomas Becket, skull and all, with all the wounds of his death, and the piece that was cut out of his skull. These bones were broken up then and there. The timber work of the shrine on the outside was covered with plates of gold, decorated with 10 or 12 rings of gold wire which contained many precious stones in them. There were also brooches, images, angels, precious stones and great pearls from the East. The materials from the shrine, the gold and precious stones, filled two great chests such as six or seven strong men could do no more than carry one of them out of the church."

"This is a description of the destruction of Becket's tomb. It was written by John Stowe in 1539"

Henry VIII and Canterbury

In the late 1520's King Henry VIII quarrelled with the Pope. He would not allow Henry to divorce his first wife, **Catherine of Aragon**. In 1533–4 Henry decided to break away from the Roman Catholic Church. He became the '**Supreme Head**' of the new **Church of England**. Two years later he began closing down all the monasteries, friaries and nunneries in the country. This had a huge impact on Canterbury.

In 1537 St Gregory's Priory was closed. Most of its buildings were demolished. St Augustine's Abbey, one of the wealthiest monasteries in England, was closed the next year. Its lands became the King's property. The Abbot's lodgings were turned into a new royal palace. Most of the other buildings were demolished. The stone from the walls and lead from the roofs were sold off. In 1538 St Sepulchre's Nunnery and the Grey, White and Black Friars were closed. In the same year Henry VIII declared that Thomas Becket had been a traitor. He ordered that his tomb and all pictures, statues and relics of him should be destroyed. Then in 1540 the Cathedral Priory, the third richest monastery in the country, was closed. The Cathedral itself was not damaged, but some of the Priory buildings were destroyed.

Sir Thomas More

Thomas More was a London lawyer. He became friendly with King Henry VIII. In 1529 he was appointed Lord Chancellor and was one of Henry's closest advisors. In 1532 he resigned because he could not accept Henry's divorce or his break from the Catholic Church. He was executed in 1535. His daughter Margaret had married William Roper from Canterbury. She brought her father's head to Canterbury. It was buried in St Dunstan's Church. 400 years later, in 1935, the Pope made More a saint.

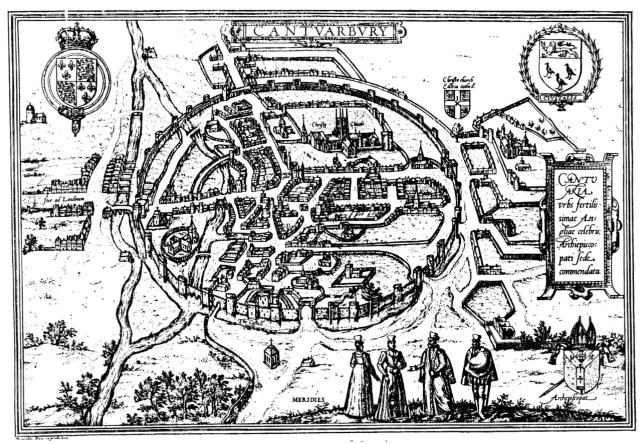

"This map of Canterbury was drawn in the middle of the 16th century."

"In 1576 William Lambard visited Canterbury. This is what he wrote about what he saw:"

Others were adapted for new uses. Twenty-four Cathedral monks lost their jobs and were given pensions. In 1541 Henry set up a new Dean and Chapter of 12 churchmen and 28 of the former monks, to look after the Cathedral and all the land it owned. He also opened a new grammar school called the King's School for 50 boys and 2 teachers.

In just 3 years Canterbury had lost Becket's shrine as well as its monasteries, friaries and nunnery. This was a devastating blow to a religious centre like Canterbury. It took many years for the city to recover.

"Canterbury is in these days in a manner waste. God has never spared his vengeance on places where his name was dishonoured. So Canterbury came suddenly from great wealth and many beautiful buildings to extreme poverty and decay ..."

"Medieval Canterbury was never the same again after the Black Death of 1349."

"The Middle Ages ended in 1485 so Medieval Canterbury must have ended then."

"Henry VIII really brought Medieval Canterbury to an end."

"When do you think that your journey to Medieval Canterbury should finish?"

A MURKY MEDIEVAL MYSTERY

Now it is your turn to work like an archaeologist. Your investigation is based on a real excavation which took place in Canterbury in 1997. You are the Director of Excavations. You have a team of archaeologists working for you. They have been working near the River Stour in Beer Cart Lane. They have found the chalk floor of a medieval building. Then they dug underneath the floor, where the soil was waterlogged. There they found a deep rectangular pit. They decided to investigate what it contained...

"Waterlogged soil helps to preserve organic materials – like the remains of plants and animals."

To solve this mystery you have to decide:

✔ what the pit was used for;

✔ and if its contents can tell us anything about the lives of people in Medieval Canterbury.

The finds

At first, the pit did not seem to be particularly interesting at all. It was full of very rich, dark soil. Then your team found these objects:

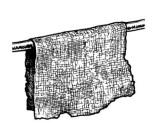

"We found this small piece of cloth in the pit. It was made in the 11th or 12th century."

"We found this broken cooking pot at the bottom of the pit. It was made at Tyler Hill, near Canterbury, in Norman times."

One of your team is an Environmental Archaeologist. She is an expert who examines soil to find remains of plants and animals. She can identify different types of bones and seeds. She took some samples of soil from the pit and studied them very carefully.

She found lots of tiny remains in the soil. This is what she found:

"Nearly 80% of the finds consisted of fruits. Plum stones were the most common."

"I also found some vole and mouse bones – and some frog bones. These animals probably fell into the pit and died there."

Understanding the finds:

People in the past dug pits for several reasons. Your team is discussing what this pit could have been used for:

"The pit could have been a grave."

"But there is no body."

"It could have been a rubbish pit. In the Middle Ages people dug pits in their gardens to put their rubbish in."

"Wouldn't a rubbish pit contain more broken pottery, large animal bones and broken tools?"

"I think the most important clues are the rich, dark soil and all the tiny remains of food..."

What I found in the soil:

FRUIT SEEDS AND STONES
Lots of plum, bullace and damson stones
Raspberry seeds
Grape pips
Apple pips
Cherry stones
Wild strawberry seeds
Elderberry seeds
Blackberry seeds
Sloe stones

VEGETABLE REMAINS
Beans
Peas
Celery
Leek
Onion
A few wheat, barley and oat grains
Lots of cereal bran (used for making bread)

TRACES OF HERBS
Dill
Opium poppy
Black mustard

ANIMAL REMAINS
Tiny chewed fish bones (mainly herring and eel)
Eggs of worms which live in human intestines
Human lice, woodlice and fleas
Beetles (including some which infest peas and beans)
A membrane from an eggshell

OTHER FINDS
Part of a hazelnut shell
A few fragments of charcoal

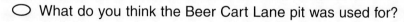

○ What do you think the Beer Cart Lane pit was used for?

○ How old is it?

○ What can you tell from its contents about the lives of people who lived in Medieval Canterbury?

CAN YOU USE THE CLUES TO SOLVE THE MYSTERY?

45

THE LEGACY OF MEDIEVAL CANTERBURY

When someone dies they leave things behind them for other people – such as memories, money and possessions. We call this their **legacy**. Medieval Canterbury 'died' about 500 years ago but its legacy still affects life in the city today. The illustrations below show some of the things which we have inherited from the people of Medieval Canterbury:

Many of Canterbury's streets still follow the routes of medieval streets. For example, this bend in Palace Street dates from the 11th century when Lanfranc took over land here to build his new Archbishop's Palace.

The medieval s⋯ of architecture became very popular again i⋯ 19th century. S⋯ Victorian buildir⋯ in Canterbury h⋯ 'medieval style' battlements an⋯ pointed arches. This is Lloyds B⋯ in the High Str⋯

The position of the Medieval walls still dominates the shape and the route of the roads of the modern city.

Thousands of people visit the⋯ Canterbury Ta⋯ in St Margaret⋯ Street every y⋯ Using models, lighting techni⋯ and the voices⋯ actors, moder⋯ visitors can joi⋯ Chaucer's pilg⋯ on their journe⋯ Canterbury ar⋯ hear five of th⋯ tales.

There were many markets in Medieval Canterbury. Street markets are still held in Canterbury on Wednesdays and Fridays.

Over two million tourists come to Canterbury every year. Like medieval pilgrims, most of them come to visit the Cathedral – as well as the other medieval buildings in the city.

You can see ⋯ reminders of Geoffrey Chau⋯ in Canterbury today, like this hotel. One of Canterbury's secondary sch⋯ the Chaucer Technology School, is also named after h⋯

Some of Canterbury's schools can trace their beginnings back to the Middle Ages. This is King's School. It was founded by King Henry VIII in 1541 and is one of the oldest schools in Italn. Simon Langton, a 13th century archdeacon at the Cathedral, left a large sum of money to the Poor Priests' Hospital. In 1881, some of it helped to fund the Canterbury 'Middle Schools'. Later they became known as the Simon Langton Grammar Schools.

There are still many medieval buildings in Canterbury. This one is in Ivy Lane.

New uses have been found for some of the buildings of Medieval Canterbury. St Alphege Church in St Alphege Street was built in the 14th century. It is now used as the Canterbury Environment Centre.

BURGATE
MERCERY LANE
PALACE STREET
GUILDHALL STREET
THE FRIARS
CASTLE STREET
ST PETER'S LANE
NUNNERY FIELDS

Many of Canterbury's moden street-names come from the Middle Ages. They were often named after the kind of people who worked in the street or important buildings which the street led to.

Canterbury has been an important religious centre since St Augustine came here just over 1400 years ago. Canterbury Cathedral was built during the Middle Ages and the Archbishop of Canterbury is still the most important churchman in England.
Photo: J. Rosenthal

Today there is a long distance footpath called the Pilgrims' Way. It starts in Winchester and ends at Canterbury Cathedral, a distance of over 100 miles (160 km). Many people walk along it to Canterbury every year following the footsteps of medieval pilgrims. Many roads in south-eastern England are called the Pilgrims' Way because they follow part of this route.

The people of Canterbury were first allowed to appoint a Mayor, elect a town council and hold law courts by medieval kings.
© David Manners.

Many of our modern surnames come from the jobs people did during the Middle Ages.

HOW TO FIND OUT MORE ABOUT MEDIEVAL CANTERBURY

Where to see remains of Medieval Canterbury

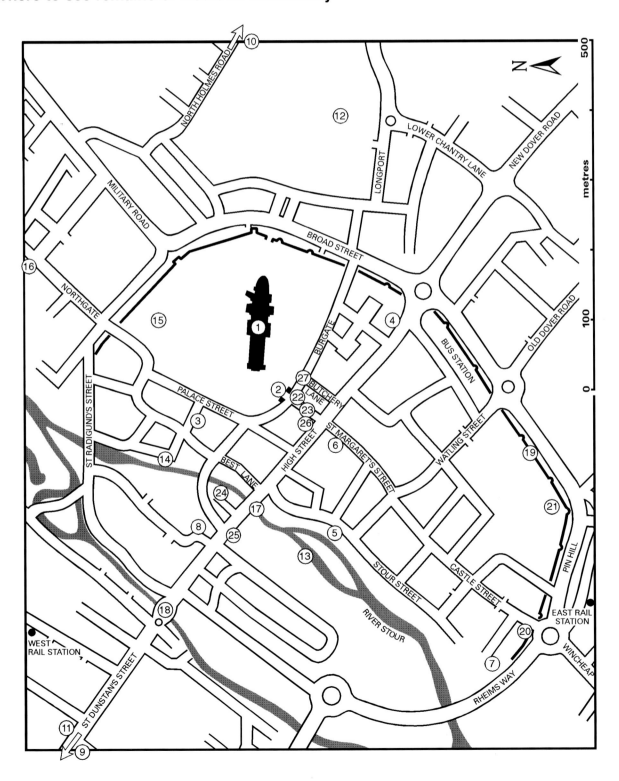

1 Canterbury Cathedral: You can see the Norman crypt, 12th century quire, 15th century nave, the site of Thomas Becket's murder and the Black Prince's tomb. Remains of the medieval priory include the cloister, chapter house and water-tower.

2 Christchurch Gate: The early 16th century gateway to the cathedral precincts.

3 St Alphege Church: This 14th century church is now used as The Canterbury Environment Centre. Events and exhibitions about Canterbury's history and the city in the 21st century, are held here.

4 St George's Clock Tower: This 15th century tower is all that remains of a medieval church which was destroyed by bombing during the Second World War.

5 Canterbury Heritage Museum: Exhibits and displays about Canterbury's history are housed in the 14th century Poor Priest's Hospital.

6 The Canterbury Tales: A lively reconstruction of 14th century pilgrims travelling from London to Canterbury. Five of Chaucer's tales are told during the journey. It is housed in St Margaret's church which largely dates from the 12th century.

7 St Mildred's Church: An Anglo-Saxon church which was rebuilt in the 13th century.

8 St Peter's Church: dates from the early Norman period.

9 St Dunstan's Church: Originally an Anglo-Saxon Church, the present church was built from the 12th to the 16th centuries. Sir Thomas More's head was buried in the church.

10 St Martin's Church: This is the oldest parish church in England. It was first built in the late 6th century but contains even earlier Roman work.

11 The Roper Gate: A 16th century brick gateway which once led to the home of the Roper family.

12 St Augustine's Abbey, Longport: The oldest monastery in this country. There are extensive remains of late Anglo-Saxon and Medieval buildings and a new museum.

13 The Greyfriars: Only the 14th century guest house survives from this medieval friary.

14 The Blackfriars: The 14th century guest hall and 13th century refectory can still be seen.

15 The Norman Staircase: This rare example of a 12th century staircase is now part of King's school.

16 St John's Hospital, Northgate: The dormitory, chapel and toilet block of this 11th century hospital can still be seen.

17 The Eastbridge Hospital: Dates from 1180. Poor pilgrims stayed here.

18 The West Gate: There were six gates in Medieval Canterbury's city walls. Only the Westgate survives today. It was built in the 1380's. It houses a museum which contains medieval weapons, armour and prison cells.

19 The City Walls: The best surviving section of Canterbury's medieval walls dates from the late 14th century

20 The Norman Castle: The large stone keep was built in the 1090's, and is now open to the public.

21 The Dane John Mound, Dane John Gardens: The mound of William the Conqueror's motte and bailey castle. It was altered in the 18th century.

22 The Buttermarket: A medieval market place.

23 Mercery Lane: A good example of a narrow medieval street with overhanging wooden buildings.

24 All Saints' Court: A 15th century timber-framed merchant's house. It is now the Mary Woodman School of Dance

25 Cogan House: Remains of Canterbury's earliest surviving stone house. It was first built in about 1200 but has been greatly altered over the centuries. It is now a restaurant.

26 The Cheker of the Hope: The stone arches from the ground floor of this 14th century pilgrim inn can still be seen in the modern shop which is on this site today.

27 The Sun Inn and Bull Inn: These two 15th century pilgrim inns are close to the Cathedral. They are now a hotel, restaurant and shops.

Street Names

Many of the street names in modern Canterbury provide important clues about its medieval past. Now that you have read this book, you should be able to identify many of them when you walk around the city.

An Archaeological Dig

The Canterbury Archaeological Trust carries out excavations in Canterbury and other parts of Kent. Medieval remains are usually uncovered. Visiting a 'dig' is a good way of seeing how archaeologists work and understanding how new evidence about the past is discovered. An archaeologist will usually be able to talk to you about what has been found. Where possible, school groups are given a guided tour of the excavation and an opportunity to see some finds. There are Work Experience placements for older students. If you are over 16 years of age you may be able to do voluntary work on an excavation.

For further information contact: Canterbury Archaeological Trust, 92a Broad Street, Canterbury http://www.canterburytrust.co.uk • tel: 01227 462062 • email: admin@canterburytrust.co.uk

Books and Other Materials about Medieval Canterbury

Canterbury Cathedral Explorer's Guide, for children, Rosemary Walters and John McIlwain. (Pitkin Guides,1997)

Becket, Oliver Postgate and Naomi Linnell. A beautifully illustrated modern version of Thomas Becket's life and death (Kingfisher Books, 1989).

A selection from The Canterbury Tales, retold by Selina Hastings (Walker Books, 1988).

The Canterbury Tales, retold by Geraldine McCaughrean (Puffin,1996).

Medieval Trail, activity booklet and guided walk around some of Canterbury's medieval remains. (The Canterbury Environment Centre,1989).

Monk's Trail, information about the lives of medieval monks in the Cathedral Priory. (Canterbury Cathedral Education Centre, 1986).

Roman and Medieval Canterbury, a historical map and guide to Roman and medieval remains in the city (Ordnance Survey, 1990).

Seven Buried Canterbury Tales, Marjorie Lyle. Seven stories based on objects found by archaeologists in Canterbury. Local bookshops or the author at 25 Rough Common Road, Canterbury CT2 9DL.(1996).

Thomas Becket: His Last Days, William Urry. An in-depth study (for older students and adults) about the events which led to Becket's murder (Sutton Publishing, 1999).

How to find out more about the Middle Ages

Books

An enormous number of books have been written about the Middle Ages. Here we have listed some books which we particularly recommend you to read if you want to find out more about the main topics in this book. Some of them might be in your school library. Otherwise your local library and bookshop will be able to help you. Make sure that you give them the title, author and publisher (shown in brackets) of the book you are interested in.

The Black Death and Peasants' Revolt, Leonard Cowie (Documentary History Series, Wayland, 1971).

Building the Medieval Cathedrals, Percy Watson (Cambridge University Press, 1976).

Discovering Medieval Realms, Schools History Project (John Murray, 1991).

Exploring a Castle, Brian Davison and Peter Dennis (Kingfisher, 1992).

Family Life in Medieval Britain, Tessa Hosking (Wayland, 1994).

Food and Feasts in the Middle Ages, Imogen Dawson (Wayland, 1994).

Life in a Medieval Monastery, Anne Boyd (Cambridge University Press, 1987).

The Growth of a Medieval Town, Dulcie Duke (Cambridge University Press, 1988).

Medieval Britain, Robin Place (Wayland, History in Evidence series, 1992).

Medieval Britain series, Peter Chrisp: **The Norman Conquest, Medieval Monarchs, Life in Medieval Britain, The Medieval Church** (Wayland)

Medieval Life, John Guy (Snapping Turtle Guide, Ticktock Publishing, 1995).

Medieval Life, Andrew Langley (Eyewitness Guides, Dorling Kindersley, 1996).

Medieval Markets, Barry Steel (Beginning History series,Wayland, 1993).

Medieval Pilgrims, Alan Kendall (Documentary History Series, Wayland, 1970).

Norman Castles, Graham Rickard (Beginning History series,Wayland, 1989).

CD-ROM

Medieval Realms, a CD-ROM containing hundreds of medieval sources including manuscripts, maps, artefacts, buildings and sites. Published by the British Library. Your school may have a copy.

Exploring Castles, contains photographs, drawings and replay sequences to help you find out about life in medieval castles, how they were attacked and defended. Available from English Heritage, PO Box 229, Northampton, NN6 9RY (tel 01604 781163).

The Internet

Internet Medieval Sourcebook: a huge collection of medieval documents. http://www.fordham.edu/halsall/sbook.html

Invasion of England, 1066: the events of 1066 and scenes from the Bayeux Tapestry. http://www.ibiscom.com/bayeux.htm

Middle Ages: an informative site which examines what it was really like to live in the Middle Ages. http://www.learner.org/exhibits/middleages

Thomas Becket: information about Becket's life and murder. http://loyno.edu/~letchie/becket/

Videos

The Battle of Hastings, The Norman Conquest of England, The Master Builders (how medieval cathedrals were built), **Looking at an Abbey** and **Looking at a Castle.** Available from English Heritage, PO Box 229, Northampton, NN6 9RY (Tel 01604 781163). Your teacher can arrange a free loan of these videos for your school.

The Silent Years: a day in the life of a medieval monk, Simon Webster and Richard Sargeant.

Available from Profile Services, 27 Forest Lane, Harrogate, North Yorkshire HG2 7HB (Tel 0143 880079).

Posters and Wallcharts

Looking at Castles and **The English Parish Church**. English Heritage, PO Box 229, Northampton, NN6 9RY (Tel 01604 781163).

The Middle Ages (Ticktock Publishing Ltd).

How to find out more about Archaeology

Books

Archaeology, Jane McIntosh (Eyewitness Guides, Dorling Kindersley, 1994).

Clues from the Past, Robin Place (Wayland, 1995).

Digging up the Past, Various authors, a series about famous archaeological discoveries (Wayland).

Landmarks from the Past, Gillian Clegg (Wayland,1994).

Now Then, Digging up the Past, Francis Pryor and David Collison (Batsford, 1993).

The Young Oxford Book of Archaeology, Norah Maloney (Oxford University Press, 1996).

The Young Scientist Book of Archaeology, Barbara Cook and Struan Reid (Osborne,1984).

CD-ROM

Introduction to Archaeology, investigating clues to discover the identity of a skeleton which archaeologists have found. Available from: AVP, School Hill Centre, Chepstow, Monmouthshire NP6 5PH (tel 01291 625439).

The Internet

Archaeology Adventure: learn how archaeologists find ancient ruins. http://tqd.advanced.org/3011/home.htm

Time Team: The site of this popular series contains lots of information about archaeology and excavations all over the country. http://www.channel4.com/plus/timeteam/

Videos

English Heritage 'Archaeology at Work' series. Titles include **Looking for the Past/Uncovering the Past, Investigating Towns, Cathedral Archaeology, Examining the Past** and **The Archaeological Detectives**. Available from: English Heritage, PO Box 229, Northampton, NN6 9RY (tel 01604 781163). Your teacher can arrange a free loan of these videos for your school.

Organisations

The Young Archaeologists' Club. This is the junior branch of the Council for British Archaeology. It has local branches all over the country. It is open to all 9–16 year olds who are interested in Archaeology. Members receive a certificate, badge, a membership card and the magazine 'Young Archaeologist'. This is published four times a year and contains reports about archaeological digs throughout the world, book reviews, news of special events, ideas for things to do and competitions. The YAC arranges visits, talks and holidays for its members. It also sends them details about the special events which are held all over the country for National Archaeology Day. Contact: The Young Archaeologists' Club, Bowes Morrell House, 111 Walmgate, York YO1 2UA (tel 01904 7671417). http://www.britarch.ac.uk/yac/

British Archaeology Students. This organisation is similar to the YAC but is for 16–21 year olds. There are two branches. The Northern Branch is run by Paul Spokes at Durham University. Write To: British Archaeology Students, 46 Saddler Street, Durham DH1 3NU.

The Southern Branch is run by Geoffrey Coles from the Surrey Heath Archaeology Trust. Write to: British Archaeology Students, 4–10 London Road, Bagshot, Surrey GU19 5HN.

Kent Archaeological Society. Young people and adults interested in the archaeology and history of Kent can join the KAS. Members receive the annual journal **Archaeologia Cantiana** and a newsletter four times a year containing information about excavations in the county, visits, study days and talks. Write to: The Honorary General Secretary, Kent Archaeological Society, Three Elms, Woodlands Lane, Shorne, Gravesend, Kent DA12 3HH.

Friends of Canterbury Archaeological Trust. This organisation keeps its members up to date with the Trust's activities. Members receive an Annual Report and a Newsletter four times a year about current excavations, excursions, lectures, volunteer opportunities etc. Write to: The Membership Secretary, Friends of Canterbury Archaeological Trust, 92a Broad Street, Canterbury, Kent CT1 2LU.

ACKNOWLEDGEMENTS

The Medieval Canterbury project has given us a wonderful opportunity to present to a wide audience material generated and gathered by the Trust over a number of years. We would like to acknowledge the contribution of all those involved in the publication production.

Many thanks go to Andy Harmsworth for managing to distil a wealth of information for the period into a readily accessible form. Thanks also go to the archaeologists and historians in the field who made valuable comments on the text. The majority of the images were generated in-house by CAT's talented illustrators and photographer, the cover designed by Mark Duncan.

We would also like to thank the following contributors for their financial support:

- The John and Ruth Howard Charitable Trust

- The Friends of Canterbury Archaeological Trust

- Albert Reckitt Foundation

- Canterbury Archaeological Trust Appeal Fund

CREDITS

Conceived, planned and written by: Andy Harmsworth

Project management by: Marion Green

Editing by: Marion Green and members of CAT Publications Committee

Picture research by: Andy Harmsworth, Marion Green and Margaret Sparks

Illustrations by: Rupert Austin, Dominique Bacon, John Atherton Bowen, Mark Duncan, Will Foster, Sue Hodgkins, Ivan Lapper, Beverly Leader, Laurie Sartin

Photography by: Andrew Savage and CAT

Canterbury Archaeological Trust manages the Archaeology in Education Service working primarily for Kent schools. The support in particular of the Kent Archaeological Society, Kent County Council Education and Canterbury City Council in this venture is much appreciated.